"Jerry C. Jaffe is a passionate expert on comedy in this deep dive of how the craft has evolved post-9/11. From how comedians addressed the tragedy to the role of wit in fighting religious fundamentalism, he writes fearlessly about fearless writers. His literary, comedic, and pop cultural reference points are mind-bending in this wide-ranging analysis on the tragically misunderstood art of satire."

– **John Fugelsang**, *SirusXM*

"Jerry C. Jaffe's *Religious Satire in the Era of New Atheism* is an accessible and entertaining look at the ways comedians grappled with religion in the wake of September 11. Jaffe's primary focus is an elucidation of the rhetorical devices that humorists use to lampoon religious fundamentalism. Along the way, though, Jaffe also sheds light on the contours of the many debates about religion in the twenty-first century. The book is recommended for anyone with an interest in contemporary satire or religion."

– **David Gillota**, author of *Dead Funny: The Humor of American Horror*

Religious Satire in the Era of New Atheism

Religious Satire in the Era of New Atheism presents a contemporary account of religious satire as evidenced by the modern art of stand-up comedy.

Focused on the context of the post-9/11 American culture phenomenon, sometimes referred to as the New Atheism – as embodied by public intellectuals such as Christopher Hitchens, Sam Harris, and Richard Dawkins – it documents the rise of comedic satire in relation to evangelical beliefs and religious dogma. Drawing on the author's own experience of stand-up performance, it examines the comedy of figures such as Mark Maron, Bill Maher, and Ricky Gervais and presents material from interviews with comedians including Lewis Black, John Fugelsang, and Leigh Ann Lord to provide unique insights into some of the issues and definitions surrounding satire.

With attention to the demonstrable rise in religious satire following the events of September 11, 2001, the author considers the clear link between this increase and the New Atheist movement, exploring shared themes and presence at specific events, such that stand-up comedy represents the Avant Garde of the New Atheists.

Jerry C. Jaffe is Professor of Theater at Lake Erie College. He has directed or performed in over 100 shows. Before coming to Lake Erie College, Jerry lived and worked in Japan and New Zealand, teaching, acting, and directing there. Many of his articles on the theater have been published in various academic journals, including "'I needed to go to this tabernacle of ignorance': Marc Maron's critique of the Creation Museum" (*Bulletin for the Study of Religion*, Vol. 42, No. 3 (2013)); and he co-edited the 2008 book *Performing Japan: Contemporary Expressions of Cultural Identity*. Recent productions he has directed include *The Memo, The Merry Wives of Windsor, Crave, Murder by Poe, Sexual Perversity in Chicago, The Jungle Book, Proof,* and *Almost, Maine*. He also performs stand-up comedy professionally, in venues around the country.

The Cultural Politics of Media and Popular Culture
Series Editor: C. Richard King, *Columbia College Chicago, USA*

Dedicated to a renewed engagement with culture, this series fosters critical, contextual analyses and cross-disciplinary examinations of popular culture as a site of cultural politics. It welcomes theoretically grounded and critically engaged accounts of the politics of contemporary popular culture and the popular dimensions of cultural politics. Without being aligned to a specific theoretical or methodological approach, *The Cultural Politics of Media and Culture* publishes monographs and edited collections that promote dialogues on central subjects, such as representation, identity, power, consumption, citizenship, desire and difference.

Offering approachable and insightful analyses that complicate race, class, gender, sexuality, (dis)ability and nation across various sites of production and consumption, including film, television, music, advertising, sport, fashion, food, youth, subcultures and new media, *The Cultural Politics of Media and Popular Culture* welcomes work that explores the importance of text, context and subtext as these relate to the ways in which popular cultures work alongside hegemony.

Also available in the series:

Isn't it Ironic?
Irony in Contemporary Popular Culture
Edited by Ian Kinane

Representing Aboriginal Childhood
The Politics of Memory and Forgetting in Australia
Joanne Faulkner

Religious Satire in the Era of New Atheism
Do You 'Seriously Believe That' After 9/11
Jerry C. Jaffe

For more information about this series, please visit: www.routledge.com/The-Cultural-Politics-of-Media-and-Popular-Culture/book-series/ASHSER-1395

Religious Satire in the Era of New Atheism
Do You 'Seriously Believe That' After 9/11

Jerry C. Jaffe

LONDON AND NEW YORK

First published 2025
by Routledge
4 Park Square, Milton Park, Abingdon, Oxon OX14 4RN

and by Routledge
605 Third Avenue, New York, NY 10158

Routledge is an imprint of the Taylor & Francis Group, an informa business

© 2025 Jerry C. Jaffe

The right of Jerry C. Jaffe to be identified as author of this work has been asserted in accordance with sections 77 and 78 of the Copyright, Designs and Patents Act 1988.

All rights reserved. No part of this book may be reprinted or reproduced or utilised in any form or by any electronic, mechanical, or other means, now known or hereafter invented, including photocopying and recording, or in any information storage or retrieval system, without permission in writing from the publishers.

Trademark notice: Product or corporate names may be trademarks or registered trademarks, and are used only for identification and explanation without intent to infringe.

British Library Cataloguing-in-Publication Data
A catalogue record for this book is available from the British Library

ISBN: 9781032536316 (hbk)
ISBN: 9781032536323 (pbk)
ISBN: 9781003412854 (ebk)

DOI: 10.4324/9781003412854

Typeset in Times New Roman
by Apex CoVantage, LLC

Contents

Acknowledgments   *viii*

1 Introduction: "I Survive Trauma Through My Sense of Humour"   1

2 Reading Between the Lines and Defining Satire: "Seeming Seeming"   12

3 Religious Satire and Doubting Thomases: "I'm Here Promoting – Doubt"   25

4 Acting Out the Character of God: "Ridiculing the Incarnation"   37

5 Comedians Satirizing Creationists: "I Needed to Go to This Tabernacle of Ignorance"   54

6 Conclusion: "People Snapped"   67

Select Bibliography   *76*
Index   *79*

Acknowledgments

The support group that is required to finish a project like this is immense. Lake Erie College provided support, and I wish to thank Deans Tom Davis and Jennifer Swartz-Levine, as well as Vice President Bryan Depoy. Routledge has a fantastic editorial staff, and I would like to thank the hard work and wise counsel of Rich King and Neil Jordan. I have had the good fortune to make numerous conference presentations on elements related to this work and would especially like to thank my colleagues and friends at the PCA National Conference and the Ray Brown Conference held at Bowling Green State University. Portions of Chapter 5 originally appeared as "'I needed to go to this tabernacle of ignorance': Marc Maron's critique of the Creation Museum." *Bulletin for the Study of Religion*, Vol. 42, No. 3 (2013). In addition to the many comedians who contributed, directly or indirectly, to this work, I would also like to thank my family Yukiko, Kayleigh, Sabrina, Soren, and Fred.

1 Introduction
"I Survive Trauma Through My Sense of Humour"

After the last commercial break of Lewis Black's April 22, 2002, performance of *Comedy Central Presents*, his final segment included this rant:

> "People snapped after September 11th . . . the one who truly snapped, the leader of the snapped, was Jerry Falwell . . ." (Black then describes how Falwell claimed that God allowed the attack to happen because of pagans and feminists. . . .) "That's odd, cause God had called me 12 hours before and he said that the reason He was upset was because of people like Jerry Falwell."

Black then goes on to make this observation about the terrorists, "that's a group that does not have a sense of humour." He contrasts that with himself, when near the end of his set, he reflects "If I learned anything from September 11 it was that I survive trauma through my sense of humour. That's how I deal with it, that's how it works for me."

Part of what makes this performance significant is that it was the first original episode of *Comedy Central Presents* that aired after the events of September 11, 2001. Actually, season 5 was already in mid-broadcast in September 2001, and the first episode broadcast was Zach Galifianakis (S5E12 original air date September 17, 2001). But this would have been recorded months earlier, and Galifianakis's routine in no way referenced the events of September 11. I conducted a review of *Comedy Central Presents* comparing seasons 3–5 to 6–7, which followed the events of September 11. Doing so allowed me to observe the amount of comments and jokes about religion before and after the attack. I tracked each comedian's performance, counting any mention of religion. For example, in the 35 episodes of seasons 3–5, only 14% of the comedians mentioned their own religious affiliations, while in the 39 episodes from seasons 6 and 7, this number was 31%. Along similar lines, any metric related to religious jokes went up in the second, post 9/11 group.

That life in the United States as well as globally changed on the morning of September 11, 2001, is a plain fact of life. The ramifications were many and

DOI: 10.4324/9781003412854-1

widespread, practical and philosophical, and at every turn tragic. Given the gravity of the events and the monumental nature of their aftermath, it may at first glance seem inappropriate to some to notice that one large and important aspect of life that was affected was the world of comedy. In the immediate aftermath, many of America's leading outlets for comedic expression took a hiatus. The most famous example may have been Jon Stewart whose *The Daily Show* remained off the air for nine days. On September 20, he returned to the air.

> Visibly shaken by the tragic events, the lives lost, the damage done, and the fear the terrorists created, Stewart returned nine days after 9/11. "They said to get back to work," Stewart said. "And there were no jobs for a man in the fetal position, under his desk crying, which I gladly would've taken. So, I come back here."
>
> (*Business Insider* August 6, 2015)

Stewart, of course, was by no means the only example. Other stalwarts of American comedy, such as David Letterman and *The Onion*, took breaks from their outputs. Joking did not completely cease however. In "'Where was King Kong when we needed Him?' Public Discourse, Digital Disaster Jokes, and the Functions of Laughter after 9/11," Giselinde Kuipers explains that Americans did not stop laughing on September 11 and provides many examples of internet jokes about the attack, including some incorporating cinema's King Kong.

Late-night comedy confronted the post-September 11 world and America's concurrent "War on Terror." S. Robert Lichter et al. provide a statistical snapshot of this trend. In 2008,

> Of the five leading late night hosts (Leno, Letterman, O'Brien, Stewart, Colbert), O'Brien told the fewest (4 percent of his total jokes), while Stewart told the most (10 percent); the other three hosts averaged 5 percent of their jokes on this subject.
>
> (125)

Various factors may be at play of course, but the key finding is that this subject takes such a prominent role in their overall discourse.

Though useful here to note that joking and laughter did not cease on September 11, one phenomenon I observed is that in the years following, there has been an increase in stand-up comedians joking about – not only the tragic events of September 11 – but religion in general. For example, Lewis Black's routine mentioned above directly criticized the Muslims responsible for the attack as well as a critique of Falwell's own theocratic response to it. As represented by this example, has there been an increase in religious satire since September 11? If so, what does this increase represent?

In considering this possibility, what has emerged is not a quantitative observation as implied by the word increase as much as a recognizable moment most clearly represented by some specific comedians. Consider the most prominent example, the career of Bill Maher. There will be much more to say about Maher's humor before this book is over, but Maher himself has described his earlier humor about religion to be friendly jests. But by the time Maher makes his film *Religulous* in 2008, he consciously and intentionally uses both his status as a celebrity and his comedic acumen to skewer and deconstruct religion with much more biting aggression. He is not just joking about religion, he has points he is trying to make.

On the August 11, 2017, episode of Maher's HBO show *Real Time*, one of his guests was scientist and prominent skeptic Richard Dawkins. One notes that Dawkins is a regular panelist on Maher's show, as was Christopher Hitchens before his death in 2011. Dawkins is known for his book *The God Delusion* (2006), while Hitchens's most famous screed on religion is *God Is Not Great* (2007). Dawkins and Hitchens have been associated with fellow outspoken skeptics Sam Harris and Dan Dennett under the colloquial name of "The Four Horseman," an ironic designation meant to showcase their central role in the broader post-September 11 movement sometimes called "New Atheism."

New Atheism

> [T]he mildest criticism of religion is also the most radical and the most devastating one. Religion is man-made.
> – Christopher Hitchens (*God Is Not Great* 10)

"The early years of the twenty-first century thrust issues around religion to the forefront of public and political debate," wrote Steven Kattell, adding:

> One of the defining features of this was the emergence of a more activist form of atheism, known as the "new atheism", which sought to openly challenge and criticize religious beliefs and to promote the virtues of reason, rationality and science.

The post-September 11 zeitgeist brought with it a renewed skepticism of religion. Although the motives of the perpetrators of the attack remain both mysterious and complex, one facet that many have focused on is their religious motivation. Even religious people in general had to label them extremists and fanatics, but some of the less religious directly questioned the role of religion in these attacks. If religion played a part then would a critique of religion provide a salve? The early twenty-first century saw a burgeoning interest in atheism, agnosticism, secularism, science, and a general distrust or at least disinterest in either organized religion or religiosity in general. A 2014 Pew survey reported a doubling of the number of self-reported atheists in the United States (up to 7%) as well as nearly one-third of respondents to their surveys claiming no religious affiliations (called the "rise of the nones" for checking the box "none of the above").

Gary Wolf may have been the first to adopt the neologism "New Atheist," in his 2006 article "The Church of the Non-Believers" (*Wired* November 1, 2006, www.wired.com/2006/11/atheism/). In this essay, Wolf declared that these "New Atheists . . . have sounded this call to arms."

> We are called upon, we lax agnostics, we noncommittal nonbelievers, we vague deists who would be embarrassed to defend antique absurdities like the Virgin Birth or the notion that Mary rose into heaven without dying, or any other blatant myth; we are called out, we fence-sitters, and told to help exorcise this debilitating curse: the curse of faith.

In this article, Wolf identifies three thinkers central to his thesis: Dawkins, Harris, and Dennett. He includes interviews with all three. In the end, Wolf summarizes, "New Atheists have castigated fundamentalism and branded even the mildest religious liberals as enablers of a vengeful mob." He sees their core message as, "no matter how confident we are in our beliefs, there's always a chance we could turn out to be wrong."

None of these three provocateurs, nor any of the other advocates of this politically active brand of secularism, created the umbrella term "New Atheist" themselves. Soon Sam Harris would publish *The End of Faith* (2005) and *Letter to a Christian Nation* (2008), and the foursome would become known as the core of this New Atheism. On February 22, 2008, the Richard Dawkins Foundation released a video of the four men in conversation called *The Four Horsemen*, cementing their association as a group of thinkers. Available originally on YouTube and then later in book form (2019), the written description of the video explains, "Richard Dawkins, Daniel Dennett, Sam Harris and Christopher Hitchens sat down for a first-of-its-kind, unmoderated 2-hour discussion" (www.youtube.com/watch?v=9DKhc1pcDFM).

Additionally, many other like-minded people and organizations emerged. A cultural moment had arrived. A struggle began between those who would attempt to show religion as having no clothes, while others rose up in defense of their cherished beliefs and traditions. In the 2019 book version *The Four Horsemen*, the foreword is written by comedian Stephen Fry, who summarizes their influence, claiming that they had given voice to "the always lurking and now growing suspicion that the worst aspects of religion, from faith-healing fakery to murderous marytdom, could not be separated from the essential nature of religion itself" (xiv-xv).

Hitchens himself characterized this cultural shift in a 2007 *Vanity Fair* essay, when he wrote:

> Could there be a change in the Zeitgeist coming on? I think it's possible. A 2001 study found that those without religious affiliation are the fastest growing minority in the United States. A generation ago the words "American atheist" conjured the image of slightly cultish and loopy Murray O'Hair. But in the last two years there have been five atheist best-sellers.

This cultural zeitgeist Hitchens describes has another facet, which is the theme of this current book. Concurrently with this so-called New Atheism, another front in the battle pushing back against religious dogma found itself as a site for a good deal of action: stand-up comedy. Among the rank and file of comedians, some took up the charge of their forebears and brought a scathing critique of religion. Naturally, just as many or more comedians avoided religion as too controversial (never wanting to divide an audience!). Some of these comedians who joined in this cultural movement have well-known names, with perhaps Bill Maher first among them. He is far from alone however. Other comedians who are openly engaged in this same brand of charged comedy include Paul Provenza, Eddie Izzard, Ricky Gervais, Jim Jefferies, Tim Minchin, Sarah Silverman, Penn & Teller, as well as many more. What these comedians are doing is twofold. First, they are focusing their comedic craft onto the anti-rationalist and hypocritical elements of religion. Second, they lend their names and celebrity to the cause so to speak, including events and projects that champion rationalism and science in a way that helps raise awareness of the event or cause. You could find them performing on TV, in the clubs, and making appearances as entertaining pundits on TV, radio, podcasts, and so on.

If so-called New Atheism attempts to counter religion, if the comedians in this study use satire to critique religion, one might wonder what any of them mean by religion. Religion is a term that in some degree defies simple definition. Soren Kierkegaard considered religious faith a paradox, since it was believing in something without evidence. Dan Dennett offered a provisional starting definition for religion as, a "social systems whose participants avow belief in a supernatural agent or agents whose approval is to be sought"(9). In *Authentic Fakes*, David Chidester includes a basic review of several common ways to define religion, beginning with the general observation "as a way of thinking, as a way of feeling, and as a way of being human in relation to other humans in the community" (15). Chidester adds that this often includes an element of the supernatural.

However, one will not find any such philosophical musing among most of the comedians. Instead, most comedians focus on what they see in the behavior of their community. Comedians use their observational skills to deconstruct behavior and ideas. This is one reason why a common target among satirists is the hypocrite. The comedian does not need their own working definition of religion, politics, or any other such social function. Instead, they need only observe fellow community members who themselves claim to live by such standards then break their own dogmatic teachings. Thus, for the purposes of this study, there is no need to develop any deeper definition for religion than the comics themselves use.

Certainly, ideas such as faith and the supernatural are common topics for discussion among the New Atheists, as well as among the comedians present. Both cohorts seem to be fighting for science, for one thing. Also, mocking what they see as bad ideas is another shared strategy. Christopher Hitchens once said in an interview with Lou Dobbs, "thus the mildest criticism of religion is also the most radical and the most devastating one. Religion is man-made" (4). This aspect of religion as-they-see-it is another motivating factor, as it becomes both a shield and a criticism.

Raphael Lataster attempted to address the moving ambiguity in defining religion on the part of New Atheists in his article, "A Superscientific Definition of 'Religion' and a Clarification of Richard Dawkins' New Atheism." He explains:

> What is Religion? It is a crucial question, particularly to Religious Studies scholars, that has never been resolved, and probably never will be. Purely substantive or essentialist definitions might satisfy some adherents of the "Western" religions, but naively ignore the importance of orthopraxy.
> (110)

Lataster reviews various approaches, from theoretical definitions of religion to definitions based on practices or cultural forms. His article focuses particularly on Richard Dawkins and the various ways critics attack him for being anti-religious. It is in this context that Lataster wants to settle on a definition of religion, one that can be used to explore this charge. Furthermore, Lataster had an opportunity to interview Dawkins, and ask him directly about religion. Dawkins affirmed to Lataster that he considers himself anti-religious, "I think I would think of myself as anti-religious, yes" and that his reason for being so are "scientific reasons. I am passionately interested in the truth" (115).

Lataster offers a definition of religion which he characterizes as "superscientific," "Religion is a form of life predicated upon the reality of the superscientific" (113). In this approach, Lataster is using the word "superscientific" as a substitute for supernatural, in the sense that he is positing that religion demands interest in that which its participants believe cannot be explained by science alone. Furthermore, religions can be in a sense ranked based on how much one religion's belief system demands greater and greater reliance upon a nonscientific worldview. And finally, fundamentalists can be understood as having as extreme demand on its adherents in both idea and need for super-scientific beliefs.

When even those who self-identify as religious cannot successfully provide a stable definition, those who are adamantly trying to push back (be they atheists, New Atheists, or religious satirists) are in a reactionary position. In a sense, those critiquing hypocrisy, nonsense, or other failures, of thought or of deed, can only react to any given situation. As described throughout this book, comedy writing often uses reactions as a form of punch line, so this situation is of no detriment to the typical satirist.

Satire and the New Atheism

In an article for CNN in 2006, Simon Hooper summed up what he saw as the heart of New Atheism, writing "What the New Atheists share is a belief that religion should not simply be tolerated but should be countered, criticized and exposed by rational argument wherever its influences arise" (www.cnn.com/2006/WORLD/europe/11/08/atheism.feature/index.html). And if there is one thing comedians are good at, it is criticizing things! When the comic muse turns its attentions to social institutions, then this is what people call satire. Though the focus here is on religious satire, naturally any facet of life can be critiqued in like manner. From the Greeks and Romans, to William Shakespeare and Ben Jonson, to Carlin and Pryor, comedy has always played the role of cultural critic. Comedians shine the mirror of distortion upon the face of reality and then mock the resulting image. Greek satire consisted of lampooning, taking the notions of others and exaggerating them in a form of *reducto ad absurdum* until the resulting version created laughter while revealing the absurdity of the original idea. George Carlin used his razor-sharp wit to deconstruct words and concepts until their underlying banality was also revealed.

> And why is it no one says, "I think he's down there now, smiling up at us?" Apparently it never occurs to people that their loved ones might be in hell. Your parents could be in hell right now . . . your father for sure. Ah shit, hell is full of dads.

This example shows the idea of taking the well-known concept of Hell and shining a mirror on the observation that some people believe in Hell but usually do not imagine their own parents in it.

This sense of comedy that is lobbying for social change brings back to mind the New Atheist movement discussed earlier. Just as New Atheists seem to believe that religion "should be countered, criticized and exposed by rational argument wherever its influence arises," thus the theme of this book is comedians who use religious satire as a way to combat the influences of religion in a post-September 11 world. One might distinguish between the friendly barbs Maher described of his earlier comedy and a more biting style of satire. In this sense, proper satire almost always includes identifying hypocrisy or contradictions in the ruling order. In order to explore this, a more careful definition of satire is required. This will be provided in the next chapter.

Comedians identify hypocrisy and use comedic rhetorical devices to lampoon religion's dogmatic intentions. For example, on the May 13, 2011, episode of *Real Time with Bill Maher*, Maher quips:

> I'm just saying logically, if you ignore every single thing Jesus commanded you to do, you're not a Christian, you're just auditing. You're not Christ's followers, you're just fans. And if you believe the earth was given to you to kick ass on while gloating, you're not really a Christian, you're a Texan.

This concise joke clearly ridicules the idea of someone who calls themselves religious but doesn't act as such. Maher is attacking the hypocrisy.

Over the years that I have been studying religious satire, I have identified several common types of jokes frequently used. As rhetorical devices, all certainly predate the tragic events of September 11. On the other hand, they provide a path through the tangled and sometimes complex art of comedy in the twenty-first century. Common rhetorical strategies utilized to great effect in religious satire include act outs of God or other religious figures, jokes which directly mock the Bible, jokes that question the role of suffering in any divine plan, the presentation of parody religions, and enacting the figure of a Doubting Thomas, sowing doubt by asking pointed questions about faith, dogma, miracles, and so on. Each of these will be covered in turn during the course of this analysis.

An act out is whenever a comedian makes a suggestion and then presents the suggestion to their audience, *in situ* as it were. An example of this would be Robin Williams wondering what it would be like if Elmer Fudd sang a Bruce Springsteen song, and then he does it, acting out his own suggestion. In religious satire, this could be any similar joke (or skit). However, the theatrical nature of stand-up comedy allows comedians to very easily present any religious figure as a character, including the Pope, Jesus, or even God, as well as of course figures from other religions, myths, or stories. I refer to this as "Voicing the Incarnate," a phrase inspired by Monty Python's *Life of Brian*, and it is the subject of Chapter 3.

If anyone has ever attended a Sunday school class, for any religion, one may have heard a child ask the teacher, clergy, or parent in charge, "Why does God let bad things happen to good people?" These young Doubting Thomases, with their childlike simplicity, raise questions about the nature of evil and why God allows suffering. The problem of evil as a theological question is called theodicy. The "Doubting Thomas" is another satiric trope, and theodicy provides a rich field for this device. For example, Eddie Izzard (another comedian covered in more depth later in this book) once asked "If there really was a god, don't you think he would have flicked off Hitler's head?" The comedic potential of theodicy and the Doubting Thomas is the subject of Chapter 4.

Chapter 5 of this book presents a rhetorical position shared by both the comedians reviewed in this book which overlaps with the New Atheism project. Christopher Hitchens summarized the ignorance about science inherent in the nature of religion when he explained:

> Religion comes from a period of human prehistory where nobody ... had the smallest idea what was going on.... Today the least educated of my children knows much more about the natural order than any of the founders of religion.
>
> (*God Is Not Great* 64)

Both comics and New Atheist writers have leapt to defend science. Furthermore, both cohorts have addressed a topic that itself is one of the great cultural tensions in modern American politics and education: evolution versus creationism. Rebranded Intelligent Design, creationism is a common target of New Atheism. In *God Is Not Great*, Hitchens wrote of intelligent design, it "*is not even a theory*. In all its well-financed propaganda, it has never even attempted to show how one piece of the natural world is better explained by 'design' than by evolutionary competition" (86, his italics).

Though usually a heated debate found at school board meetings and occasionally in the courts, it turns out that a survey of modern religious satire shows that the unscientific nature of creationism is a topic comedians have tackled. For example, Marc Maron dedicated an episode of his podcast *WTF* to a visit to the Creation Museum in Petersburg, Kentucky, and then included a 15-minute routine about it on his comedy album *This Has to Be Funny* (2011). On the album, he refers to the museum as a "tabernacle of ignorance." In addition to Maron, others who have picked up on this topic include Eddie Izzard, Lewis Black, as well as Maher's film *Religulous*.

Sometimes, comedians who mock religion in their act are derided for "preaching to the choir" but it would be a mistake to underestimate the power of doing so. After all, "preaching to the choir" is exactly what churches in fact do, so there must be some benefits to the strategy. Benefits include training in secularism and logic, the power of bringing entertainment hand-in-hand with sober issues, and the community-building that shared laughter creates. Douglas E. Cowan notes that the conversational style of most stand-up comedy relies on the performer and the audience having some shared qualities, "by sharing common understandings about religion, by participating in the 'taken-for-grantedness' that makes for comedy" (36). That a comedian's

10 *Introduction*

Figure 1.1 This study explores the overlapping cultural spheres of New Atheism, September 11, and religious satire. The center overlap is where this study thrives.

audience might be cynically referred to as a choir only indicates that they may have some shared values, "understandings" which make both communication and the difficult act of humor possible.

As a final summary of this book's theme, please refer to the following diagram (Figure 1.1). This diagram illustrates the three cultural spheres referred to in this book, and as is so concisely suggested in Venn diagram form, we are exploring that middle area of overlap.

A Note on "Islamophobia"

There is also a suggestion that some space be given to a discussion of rising Islamophobia following 9/11. This is an incredibly important topic in general, but also quite germane to this project. For one thing, there is definitely a form of satire from this era which embraces Islamophobia. I remember seeing it in the clubs at the time, and there are prominent examples (Jeff Dunham's "Achmed the Dead Terrorist" comes immediately to mind). On the other hand, some of the well-known participants among both New Atheist writers and some of the comedians present have also been accused of Islamophobia. To give obvious examples, comedian Bill Maher and New Atheist writer Sam Harris have both been accused of this. Up until now, Islamophobia has not been a significant element of this study. First, it is arguably tangential, but second, these accusations involve a lot of back-and-forth between accusers and the persons, and would be hard to document in short form. The topic would deserve a book (or more!) of its own. I do include examples of Arab-American satire about 9–11, including Dean Obeidallah, The Axis of Evil comedy tour, and the documentary *The Muslims Are Coming!*, among others.

A Note on "Auto-Ethnography"

I want to alert the reader here at the beginning of this journey that one element of this study includes an auto-ethnographic approach. This is because I myself tour and perform as a stand-up comedian. (This is in addition to 40+ years in the theater in general, including Improv and sketch comedy.) My academic training demands a sense of rigor and value to the objective mindset. I think I have followed these professional expectations to a very high degree. However, I have also stood on stage and discovered which of my jokes have landed and which have bombed. I have socialized with hundreds of other comedians (from famous A-listers to the lowliest open mic'ers), watching their acts and listening to their advice and ideas. I have stayed up late drinking, cracking wise, and waxing philosophical. As such, I spend a good deal of time in comedy clubs and around comedians of every level. In addition to the thousands of shows I have seen, I have had the good fortune to meet hundreds of talented performers, and with them enjoyed many personal conversations.

Additionally, I produce and host a podcast on the subject of religious satire called *The Comical Heathen Podcast*, which includes many interviews from which I quote freely. From an anthropological perspective, I am an "insider," and it is my hope that this positioning adds to the depth of my thesis without being prisoner to blind spots that sometimes bedevil auto-ethnographic works. Also, if the osmosis that sometimes occurs when one is immersed in a cultural milieu means that I ever fail to properly credit an organic idea to a friend, colleague, mentor, or conversation, I both apologize to the offended comrade and thank them heartily for all the good times I've enjoyed on this journey. Thus, as I dutifully fill my bibliography with the most up-to-date scholarship and gather as much source material and research as I can muster, baked into this cake is my own journey in this world of comedy.

Finally, a quick explanation about my approach to citations and the bibliography readers will find at the end of this work. It is my goal to thoroughly document all of my research materials while also maintaining a smooth and easy-to-read style. With this in mind, I have divided all of my materials into two groups. Traditional print materials such as books, magazines, and newspapers are noted in the text and then included on my final bibliography. Digital, audio-visual, and podcasting references are given in-text as well but not included on the final bibliography. I hope this approach makes sense and results in an enjoyable reading experience.

2 Reading Between the Lines and Defining Satire

"Seeming Seeming"

> Ha! little honor to be much believed, And most pernicious purpose! Seeming, seeming! I will proclaim thee, Angelo.
>
> (*Measure for Measure* II iv)

"Seeming seeming" comes from Shakespeare's satire *Measure for Measure*, a play on the theme of disguise and religious hypocrisy. *Measure for Measure* is the only play by William Shakespeare to so fully address the topic of religious hypocrisy. The word "seeming" appears in the play six times, always meaning a lying false exterior and often applied to the hypocritical antagonist Angelo. While placed in charge of the city by the absent Duke, Angelo works to stamp out unlawful sexuality, threatening to punish promiscuity with death. When he falls in lust with nun-to-be Isabella, he proposes to save her brother's life if she will sleep with him in secret. Shocked by this hypocrisy in a self-proclaimed religious man, Isabella declares "Ha! little honor to be much believed, And most pernicious purpose! Seeming, seeming! I will proclaim thee, Angelo" (II iv). This example of her "seeming, seeming" accusation compactly represents all we need to know about religious satire. Angelo is a hypocrite, and Isabella exposes the difference between act and dogma. One is reminded of Moliere's *Tartuffe*, another play in which lascivious intent is disguised by pious-seeming behavior.

The long history of satire goes back at least to the golden age of Athens and her poets, playwrights, and philosophers 2,500 years ago. These writers were concerned with the difference between act and deed, and it is a topic one sees throughout Greek metaphysics and art. Classic Greece's greatest comic writer Aristophanes has 11 surviving complete plays (of perhaps 40 or so). All involve irony, and all have shades of satire. The earlier ones, such as *The Knights* (424BCE) and *The Clouds* (423 BCE), and perhaps his most famous play *Lysistrata* (411 BCE) are particularly satiric. The latter tells the story of Greek women trying anything they can to end the Peloponnesian war. They begin with a sex strike and move on to kidnapping a magistrate, staging a mock ritual, and then finally forcing the men of war to reconcile and end the

DOI: 10.4324/9781003412854-2

fighting. Though mostly seen as an anti-war play, with some proto-feminist ideas, the ritual scene itself is a parody of a religious function (see Chapter 4).

Aristophanes, Shakespeare, and Moliere help demonstrate that comedy, irony, satire, and religious satire are part of history. They are one manner of expressing the human condition. Focusing in on contemporary cultural practices, what, then, is satire? I would like to proceed with an example. While interviewing theologian Bart Ehrman on *The Colbert Report*, Stephen Colbert succinctly captures the sense of religious satire with this one simple joke: "I believe that the Bible is inerrant, without flaw, and directly from the mouth of god. Let's have a reasonable discussion" (June 20, 2006). As a joke, it is perfectly crafted. It has a premise, also called the set up – in this case, the first half of the joke: "I believe that the Bible is inerrant, without flaw, and directly from the mouth of god." The second phase of a joke is commonly known as the punch line. In a well-written joke, the punch line must extend logically from the premise but also surprise the listener with an unexpected continuation. Thus "Let's have a reasonable discussion" is simultaneously logical and incongruous. Due to the surprising nature of punch lines, they are sometimes called "the turn."

Jokes have much in common with riddles. In the case of both riddles and jokes, the second half must be both logically consistent and unexpected. Riddles of course have no requirement to be funny, although irony and word play (common features of jokes) play their part in the world of riddling. In this case, the punch line is "Let's have a reasonable discussion." This is a perfect turn. Even though the two sentiments would seem to contradict each other, thus fulfilling the surprise element of the turn, the underlying logic is sound. It is a satiric take on religious fundamentalism. Colbert enacts what Linda Hutcheon calls "the ironist" that is the one performing the irony, for whom "irony is the intentional transmission of both information and evaluative attitude other than what is explicitly presented" (105). In this manner, Colbert perfectly portrays by his performance that despite the words he uses he acknowledges that it the opposite is true – reasonable discussion is impossible with fundamentalists.

Of course, this example is not strictly speaking from the world of stand-up comedy. However, it does share another important element with stand-up. All good stand-up performances proceed from the logic of the performer's "point of view." That is, the stage persona of the comedian is what creates the logical internal consistency in the act in general and a given set of jokes in a performance. On the *Colbert Report*, Colbert was famous for his strong character point of view. Considered a parody of FOX's Bill O'Reilly, Colbert enacted a conservative talk show host while undermining it with irony. The level of sophistication in both the writing and the performance was well admired. (Also, studies have shown that the more conservative any given audience member to his show might be, the more likely they were to think Colbert really did mean what he was saying!)

In these first few examples, Shakespeare, Aristophanes, and Colbert set us on track, but can we generate a useful definition of satire? With my emphasis on stand-up comedy and interest in New Atheism, another comedian who overlaps these cultural spheres is Paul Provenza. Best known perhaps for his Showtime show *The Green Room* (2010–2011) and for directing the film *The Aristocrats* (2005), Provenza has also co-authored with Dan Dion a book of interviews with comedians called *Satiristas!* (2010). In his introduction to the book, he first offers his own take on the Classical sense of the word *satire*, which according to him means, "mocking a point of view by embracing it so fully as to allow its absurdity to become self-evident" (xx). This is consistent with the Greek word "lampooning," a form of satire in which one depicts the most extreme version of an opponent's position. This is the humorous version of *reducto ad absurdum*, the logical fallacy of refuting someone's argument "by carrying the argument to its logical end and so reducing it to an absurd conclusion" (Shermer 58). And this is perhaps the most apt description of Colbert's performance on the *Colbert Report*.

Continuing, Provenza then offers his own dictionary-style definition of satire:

*The use of Humor, irony, exaggeration, or ridicule to expose people's stupidity or vices, particularly in the context of contemporary politics or other topical issues.
   *A literary work holding up human vices or follies to ridicule or scorn.
   *Trenchant wit, irony, or sarcasm used to expose and discredit vice or folly.

(XX)

Note the practical nature of Provenza's approach. In addition to his own career as a comedian, he is well known among comedians as a historian of comedy. So, one might expect him to offer, perhaps, a more in-depth definition. Philosophical musings, of some sort? But the point is, he is a comedian, and comedy above all else is a results-oriented art form. Precise or prescient definitions are not in this wheelhouse. Provenza makes this point himself, "talking with comedians about stuff like an accurate definition of 'satire' is like talking about sound waves and frequencies with jazz cats. It's just not that relevant to what they do" (xx).

For example, this collection includes Provenza's interview with Colbert. Provenza asked him if he considered himself an influencer on politics and American culture, an idea to which Colbert expressed skepticism, or maybe disinterest. "I'm out for laughs" Colbert insisted. In reference to his performance at the 2006 White House Correspondents' Dinner, Colbert remarked, "When people came up to me after . . . and said 'Fuck those people, man. What difference does it make if they laugh?' I was like, 'No, it kind of matters to me'" (27). In an interview on my podcast *The Comical Heathen*, TV writer Marc Jaffe (who wrote several episodes of *Seinfeld*) expressed the same idea, saying "Depending on the joke, is it funny? Funny first."

In sync with the idea of the comic performer and their performance, my analysis naturally includes the filter of my own experiences as a stand-up comedian. This reminds me of something Peter McGraw said when I had the chance to interview him about the Humor Research Lab he helps run. "To crack the humour code," he told me, "you need the richness of experience, out in the real world" (*The Comical Heathen Podcast* S1 E17 2019). As a researcher, he needed to get out into the real world. As a comedian, I need to get into a lab!

> I generally grow this beard out around Christmas. Then, I like to go to malls dressed as Jesus, and what I do is generally walk through the mall, just saying, "No, no, this wasn't what it was supposed to be about, people." But if there's a Santa at the mall, I'll walk right up to him and I'll go, "Listen, fat man, you're just a clown at my birthday party."
> – Marc Maron

As explained by Northrop Frye, satire presents an "inconvenient truth: Philosophies of life abstract from life, and an abstraction implies the leaving out of inconvenient data. The satirist brings up these inconvenient data" (229). Frye goes on to demonstrate that attacks on both pseudoscience and religion have a long history in satire and comic writing. The above Marc Maron joke functions in just this way. The basic premise of Maron's line of satire is pointing out the "inconvenient data" represented by Christmas-as-consumption NOT being a part of the teachings of the biblical Jesus. Rather, contemporary consumerism in fact contradicts the recorded utterances of the biblical figure of Jesus and his disciples. In this way, for Frye and others, satire is always both judgmental and conservative. Maron's joke is certainly judgmental but it is also conservative in spirit in that it thematically reminds the listener about what the worship of Jesus is supposed to be about. (This is not to say that Maron himself is politically conservative nor particularly religious. Just that for this joke to function there must some sense of core values at play.)

Another example of this quality of satire based upon exposing missing data from someone's world view is Ian Harris's take on religious people who criticize atheist authors such as Dawkins. On his 2011 special *Critical and Thinking*, he acts out a conversation between himself and his "friend who is a Christian." The friend spots a Dawkins book in Ian's home and proclaims: "Richard Dawkins? That guy's an idiot! That guy's a moron!" As the bit continues, Ian says to his friend:

> I think he makes a hundred good arguments, I'd love to hear you refute one of them. Just one. Pick the easiest one. Pick the one that when you read

through it, you said, "this is garbage, I'm going to smash this." Give me your rebuttal, go.

The friend's reply to this, he admits, "I haven't read the book." Act outs can be a powerful way to create irony, which I cover later (see Chapter 4). But in this particular joke, the humor is also based on the inconvenient truth that frequently Christian apologists criticize atheist works without actually reading them. This joke shows a conservative cultural value in the sense that one must come prepared to a debate, not spout ignorant dogmatic statements without foundation.

Harris creates the comedic moment through his act out of the premise, which is to say he creates a narrative form. Narratives are a crucial component of postmodernism, since postmodern analysis has two essential interpretations, which are that grand master narratives have dissolved away while any attempt at epistemology or knowledge can only exist while embedded in narratives of some kind. Christopher Gilbert wrote about this in "Of Satire and Gordian Knots." On this difficult conundrum, Gilbert explained, "labeling any satire as postmodern means belying the tendency of satire to deprive its comic contempt through a narrative on narratives" (129). When applied to Maron, Harris, and many other comics found in this book, this suggests a meta-position for the artist. They are telling a story about a story in order to point out the irony of what is missing. The satirist emphasizes the inconvenient truth that belies hypocrisy, ignorance, or both.

> These are my principals. If you don't like them, I have others.
> – apocryphal but often attributed to Groucho Marx

Mikhail Bakhtin's model for communicative utterances posits that there is an existential difference between what is said or uttered AND what is heard or received and that meaning is created via the context of actual exchanges between two or more agencies. It is assumed that the original utterance was motivated by intent and that the source of each utterance had an intended meaning (or even multiple intended meanings). However, in real-life communicative events, the receiver of the utterance may have an understanding different from that of the sender. This could be a simple error in understanding, including nuance of meaning or unusual words, for example. This could be a genuine misunderstanding, but this also could be a willful misunderstanding, such as when the receiver chooses to interpret an utterance in the way that benefits themselves regardless of intended or obvious meanings. A concise example comes from *The Simpsons*, when Marge complains, "You aren't even listening to me. You're only hearing what you want to hear" and Homer replies, "Thanks honey! I'd love a pork chop right about now!"

Also, language or cultural barriers exist that make direct understanding difficult or impossible. There is a type of humor based upon this, the malapropism. A good deal of immigrant humor is based on this principal of misunderstanding. It is most clearly embodied by Chico Marx's Italian immigrant character, or more recently by Borat. There also could be contextual clues that not all participants are aware of, or perhaps varying individuals interpret differently.

The suggestion that utterances have a narrow or intended meaning is what Bakhtin means by "monologic." Utterances and language have a monologic quality, particularly in real-world communication contexts. One is trying to say something. However, this monologic tendency is only an implied feature, as in realistic communication events the actual meaning is forged case by case by all the participants on an individual basis. Each participant generates their own understanding(s) based upon this communal moment. This communal creation of multiple meanings is labeled by Bakhtin as "dialogic." In contemporary vernacular, the word *dialogue* refers to two or more people speaking and in a theatrical context refers to the written and spoken portions of a play script. But the root word is "dia-," which in Greek contains the notion of something passing between people, and it is in this more classical sense that Bakhtin uses the word dialogic. Therefore, meaning is transactional; it is something that happens between people. Of course, as the word dialogue implies speaking, we can understand that this refers to conversations, but as a model for language and communication, it also refers to all types of communicative utterances, nonverbal, written, hieroglyphic, icons, design, all types of art in every type of medium. (All teachers must be aware of the irony of trying to explain "monologic" speech, with all of our intended meanings but with the existential knowledge that it can never be understood monologically!)

Stand-up comedy has been characterized as "brave speech" and otherwise generally fearless. Folk wisdom tells us that clowns have always had leeway to mock the king. In an interview for *The Comical Heathen Podcast*, Leighann Lord explained this function while discussing George Carlin: he was always "Poking at the system, showing the flaws . . . truth-teller, town crier, the emperor has no clothes approach to comedy." Authoritative utterances attempt to fix meaning. But Bakhtin demonstrates that this is contrary to the actual functioning of language. "The word in language is half someone else's" (*The Bakhtin Reader* 77). Meaning is not fixed but rather co-created between text and reader, speaker and listener. "The word in living conversation is directly, blatantly, oriented toward a future answer-word" (*The Bakhtin Reader* 76). Thus, Bakhtinian dialogics situates meaning as co-created in the moment of social context. Certainly, believers invested in the ideas of one or another dogma may participate in perpetuating the myth of a monologic meaning, but the meaning itself is never solely in the utterance. As Michael Holquist summarizes it, "Dialogue is real, monologue is not; at worst, monologue is an illusion, as when it is uncritically taken for granted" (59). And nowhere is the illusion of truth uncritically taken for granted than in the cultural sphere of religious beliefs.

One of the contributing factors to this transactional nature of generating meaning via communicative utterances includes what Bakhtin refers to as "surplus of vision." The meaning of this phrase is also sometimes expanded to include a good deal of human psychology, but basically it refers to a very particular and oft overlooked aspect of real-life encounters between interlocutors. If you and I meet and have a conversation, if we sit at a table in a coffee shop, enjoy our beverages and innocently talk about this, that, and the other, as I look at you and you at me, each of us sees the world differently. And in this case, Bakhtin means this very literally. I see what is behind you, but you see what is behind me. Indeed, I see your face and you see mine, but neither of us sees our own faces. Thus, in a very literal sense, we are seeing the world differently than each other. This difference in vision is characterized as a "surplus" because we each see more than the other.

Besides this very literal intention of "surplus of vision," some expand the notion to include everything that is different between us. Perhaps one is male and the other female. Perhaps we are from different cities, states, or countries. Other factors may include education level, parenting, religious background, etc. As we sit down to have a simple and friendly chat, we are literally seeing two different worlds during our conversation, and we are seeing that world in different ways.

For Bakhtin, the natural consequence of one taking the concept of surplus of vision to heart is a more ethical way of being in the world. First, for practical reasons, one can consciously realize that the people around you are literally seeing the world differently, and since you are generating meaning together in this encounter, you can interact in a more thoughtful and intentional way that acknowledges this very real-world condition. On another level, acknowledging and respecting the presence of surplus of vision can increase one's empathy in the world and foster a greater feeling of shared responsibility not only for the generation of meaning but also for those with whom you generate meaning. Third, and for Bakhtin undoubtedly the most important, if one accepts that you carry this surplus of vision within you and thus you yourself are a unique way of seeing the world, then you realize that you must participate in the world in a proactive way. What you see, no one else sees. Thus, you must act, and your actions must be understood within an ethical framework.

The tension between the monologic tendency of utterances and the dialogic actuality of meaning-making is the fundamental tool of the comedian. As a performance art, the stand-up comedian is physically situated to play high status, as the audience's attention is on them. The audience is darkened, the comic lit. This social context empowers the comic. It reminds one of why Bakhtin considered theater to be a very monologic art form, overall. In *Rabelais and His World*, Bakhtin contrasts the theater with what he calls the carnival, writing,

> carnival does not know footlights, in the sense that it does not acknowledge any distinction between actors and spectators. Footlights would

destroy a carnival, as the absence of footlights would destroy a theatrical performance.

(7)

In traditional theater, the artists make most of their interpretive decisions and try to present them in an effective and moving way. In this sense, theater has a strong monologic drive. Paradoxically, stand-up comedy has its conversational aesthetic, with the comedian as cousin to the carnivalesque fool, but all the while performing in the actor's milieu of the stage. Analogous to the clown, comedians have a will to speak truth to power, engaging in dialogic play. But their performance has all the hallmarks of the theatrical. The comedian's stage is lit by the stage lights, an artificial world is created, the medium is the message, and thus, the art of stand-up is rhetorically monologic.

The comedian encounters "things" in life, from the most trivial to the most monumental, and in deciphering them, they present alternative meanings of what might have been otherwise obvious intentions. This is indeed the definition of irony, uttered by a robot called Bender in an episode of *Futurama*: "the use of words in other than their obvious intentions." Comedians must observe utterances in action in real life and find humor in dialogically, willfully challenging the intended meanings.

Satire as palimpsest – the humorist writes on top of the existing version of the story, creating changes and challenging the history that is unfolding. In pop culture studies, palimpsest usually refers to "rubbing over," that is like reused monastic scrolls which the previous writing is still vaguely visible underneath newer scribbles – any pop culture form which recycles or combines the previous with the current might receive this type of labeling or analysis. The comedian's taking the words or actions of political and religious leaders and ironically deconstructing their monologic utterances is a type of live-action palimpsest. It is a corrective that highlights the absurdity of such utterances or actions and then singles out the individuals or groups who are responsible to treat them to public ridicule. It is a corrective in the form of rubbing out parts of what was said or done and overwriting alternative and ironic interpretations which highlight the absurdity. Bad ideas are shown to be bad by the process of humorously rubbing over them.

Religion lends itself to such ridicule due to its typically one-sided rhetoric. Attempts by religious leaders to present theological dogma as precise and unerring must falter in the reality of language's own dialogical quality. Elision and misinterpretation are unavoidable, not to mention playful, willful misinterpretation. Surplus of vision demands the comic prioritize their power to do this. Comedy has the ability to skewer the dogmatic nature of religious utterance by highlighting this lack of linguistic or rational flexibility.

In *This Has to Be Funny*, Maron deconstructs the monologic narrative of the Creation Museum. For example, Maron reacts to a lamb that sits with Adam in the Museum's Garden of Eden gallery. Maron begins by noting that the Garden is well done and beautiful: he says, "The 'Garden of Eden' was beautiful. You walk in, there's animal noises, it's big, it's a garden, it's beautiful. Animals, it's just Adam." Then, the lamb: "in the middle sits Adam, alone, holding a white lamb. Which is either to foreshadow Christ . . . or he's fucking it. Either one is possible, in pre-Eve Eden." Thus, he turns the intended meaning of the lamb's presence into a willful misreading that undermines the Museum's entire biblical narrative. I will discuss Creationism (and the Creation Museum) as a target of religious satire in a future chapter, but for now, this joke exemplifies the monologic/dialogic tensions comedians exploit (see Chapter 5).

Political and religious leaders operate on the self-confident belief that their utterances are monologic. Constitutions, laws, mandates, dogma, commandments, fatwa's, excommunications, and other such official decrees are issued with maximal confidence in their monologic force. However, since communication is always actually dialogic, one can expose the transactional nature of these monologic dreams by willfully misinterpreting them. When done successfully, the comedian generates both laughter and discourse about the meaning and basis of such top-down messages.

Religious dogma is a clear example of monologic utterances. Since meaning is never fixed, it is possible for satirists to parody religious utterances. According to Henri Bergson, the comic construct transposes the mechanical on to the organic. Thus, any attempts to transfix the dialogic nature of utterances onto mechanical, monologic discourses are inherently comedic. Since the tools of comedy can so successfully demonstrate the hypocrisy of such official decrees, this also means that the project of comedy always has an ethical imperative. This is not to say that every single comedian, or comic writer, needs to think of their art as ethical, or think of themselves as ethical, or even that there is one monologic definition of who is or is not ethical. As a form of rhetoric, all comedy has the force of persuasion. Joanna Gilbert claims, "Although not as overtly rhetorical as a political stump speech or a telemarketer's spiel, performance, particularly the performance of stand-up comedy, is inherently a rhetorical act" (2). As per Provenza's practice-based considerations, comedians, on stage, under the lights, have a feel for joke-making, and it is simply not an academic enterprise at that level.

This Bakhtinian linguistic perspective is buttressed by a parallel in Bergsonian psychology. Henri Bergson theorized that people laugh at the mechanical encrusted onto the living. Mechanical thinking is opposed to the elastic force of life; he calls it the *élan vital*. Thus, just as dogmatic utterances strive for monologic authority, they are also crusty and inflexible thinking, opposed to the evolution of thought and indeed life and therefore inherently ridicule-able.

Each individual comedian's surplus of vision is what gives him or her the intellectual basis for their deconstruction of meaning. Choosing to share these unique mind droppings (as George Carlin once characterized his own jokes) is to live in the world with conscious acknowledgment of a surplus of vision. Also, there is absolutely no need for any particular comedian to know or use the vocabulary of Bakhtin, Bergson, or Frye. Professional comedians and comedy writers, working on the coasts and all points in between, and globally, work on one main principal: be funny.

As noted above, sometimes comedians make gentle comments that mildly ridicule religion, as Maher described of his early work. For example, Catholic and Jewish comedians often joke about their upbringing, household customs, and families, but without attacking religion itself. In his 2000 special on *Comedy Central Presents*, Jim Gaffigan described being Pope as a strange job ("wouldn't it have been weird to go to high school with the pope?") and described having to go to church as a Catholic and not really knowing what was being said during readings, so he found himself "paraphrasing the Bible during the reading." Similarly, Carol Leifer said that as a "thrifty" Jewish person, "minibars in hotels are nothing but a conversation piece" (*Comedy Central Presents* 2003). These are examples of mild, self-deprecating humor, with the comedian's own heritage or upbringing as the target more so than any religious dogma or hypocrisy. This could even be considered consistent with some rabbinical traditions that consider laughter an important function in religion. In "What's so funny about arguing with God? A Case for Playful Argumentation from Jewish Literature," Don Waisanen et al. emphasize, "[H]umor's capacity to bisociate between different domains of human experience and argumentation's emphases upon dissoi logoi act as structural forms of reasoning that can prevent reification." In other words, humor has a place within the debate tradition of Rabbinical studies and can be used to criticize social institutions.

One feels that real satire should have more bite than this. Artists empowered by the ethical notion of surplus of vision could well be much more disarming in their satire. In her study of contemporary politically motivated stand-up comedy *All Joking Aside*, Rebecca Kreftling notices the same differentiation. Kreftling contrasts George Carlin's earlier religious jokes with that of Bill Maher. She describes Carlin's satire as "light-hearted and good-natured as when he assumes a Brooklyn accent to play Jesus being interviewed for a radio show" (55). But later Bill Maher, she claims, "does not just criticize religion; rather, he uses charged humor to demonstrate how religious practice perpetuate inequality" (56). And comedy that is intentionally focused on aggressively critiquing social justice issues is what she calls "charged," a term Kreftling has introduced. Kreftling explains, "Charged humor springs from a social and political consciousness desiring to address social justice issues" (25). Furthermore,

> Terms such as satire, political humor, or biting humor do not quite capture the proactive qualities of charged humor, a metaphor I use to describe humor intending to incite social change, develop community, and lobby for civil rights and acknowledgements.
>
> (25)

In 2014, Sarah Silverman released a video titled "Sarah Silverman is visited by Jesus Christ" (www.youtube.com/watch?v=ahdR6aHQvMQ). Directed by Wayne McClammy, the video was released in support of a Pro Choice advocacy group then called Lady Parts Justice. The video depicts Silverman addressing the camera and explaining that Jesus came to her during the night. While explaining what she learned, which was that Jesus is actually pro-choice, an actor portraying Jesus (Michael Weatherly) also joins the skit. He tells her that he's really disappointed "by these people who use my name for intolerance and oppression." In the video, she asks Jesus "When does life begin" and he answers "At 40. (they laugh) The fertilized eggs aren't people, people are people." As a religious, satiric skit, it has an act out in the form of Jesus (putting both jokes and political points in his mouth, a rhetorical strategy discussed more in Chapter 4) and is fiercely pro-choice in its advocacy, another example of extremely charged humor as per Kreftling.

In *The Humor Code*, Peter McGraw and Joel Warner explain McGraw's Benign Violation Theory and how it helps explain comedy and the effect it has on people. A behavioral psychologist, McGraw is also known for establishing the Humor Research Lab at the University of Colorado. Through various studies and experiments there, he and colleagues have developed the thesis that "humor only occurs when something seems wrong, unsettling, or threatening (i.e., a violation), but simultaneously seems okay, acceptable, or safe (i.e., benign)" (*The Humor Code* 10). McGraw offers tickling as an example:

> tickling involves violating someone's physical space in a benign way. People can't tickle themselves . . . because it isn't a violation. Nor will people laugh if a creepy stranger tries to tickle them, since nothing about that is benign.
>
> (11)

This model sheds some light on satire as well. In some contexts, it would seem a violation to criticize the dogma of a community or their leaders (religious, political, or others such as parents, etc.). On the other hand, the context of humor creates a social space where such criticism is both normative and fun. Therefore, no matter how much of a violation a criticism seems, in a comedic context, the criticism also has a benign element. This also becomes clear when a comedian takes a joke too far, such as Rosanne Barr's Hitler cookies or Kathy Griffin's Trump head photos or Ted Danson's blackface routine at a Whoopi Goldberg roast. Even though humor may have been intended, the resulting bits were for some more of a violation with too little of the benign.

Nonetheless, the notion of the benign in satire is undoubtedly peculiar, since as Frye has pointed out, the criticism inherent in satire may be just and needed. It has normative values for the community. Additionally, specific comedians (like most of the ones in this study) may have a fan base that expects such comedians to satirize, perhaps even viciously. These elements indicate that though minimized, the benign may still be present. I discussed this exact point with McGraw on my podcast (*The Comical Heathen* podcast S1 E17 2019), during which I said, "there must be a kind of violation . . . the comedian is going to call out the church, so it would seem to heavy on violation but light on benign . . . there must be a playful clown" to which McGraw agreed: "it is okay to critique people in power. Equally important is actually the genius of the comic . . . to make this a 'humourous complaint'. To make it more playful, to make this fun."

This sense of comedy that is lobbying for social change brings back to mind the New Atheist movements discussed earlier. Just as New Atheists seem to believe, as per Simon Hooper, "that religion should not simply be tolerated but should be countered, criticized and exposed by rational argument wherever its influence arises" thus the theme of this book is comedians who use charged religious satire as a way to combat the influences of religion in a post-September 11 world. They identify hypocrisy and use dialogic rhetorical devices to lampoon religion's monologic force. For example, on the "New Rules" segment of his November 4, 2016, broadcast of *Real Time* Bill Maher does a humorous screed on how evangelic support for Donald Trump during the 2016 elections reveals their hypocrisy. "It's hard to bring up the ten commandments when your candidate spent his life breaking all of them." Maher is highlighting the hypocrisy of self-avowed religiously motivated values-voters backing a candidate with clearly no religious values. Maher points out that Trump when asked was incapable of citing even one scripture and that in a speech at religious Liberty University, he erroneously identified the New Testament chapter known as "Second Corinthians" as "Two Corinthians." Maher hits home the hypocrisy, "Jesus healed the blind, Trump mocks the handicapped. Jesus turned the other cheek, Trump grabbed her pussy."

Another example of a comedian lampooning the hypocrisy of religious language that is dogmatic and monologic is from Ricky Gervais's 2003 special *Animals* when he reads parts of the Bible out loud while playing as if it is all true. The set up for this routine begins with Gervais saying that he has found a viable alternative to the Darwin's Theory of Evolution, "it's called the Bible. Darwin was wrong, we didn't evolve, God made us." He then spends several minutes reading passages from Genesis out loud. He says at one point:

> Some of the things you'll hear do sound a little bit far-fetched, I admit that, I thought it was, but then I found the other name of the Bible is the Gospel, so it is all true, so, luckily the clue is in the title.

In a manner similar to the Colbert exchange above, in this routine Gervais acts out a "believer" who wants us to take the Bible literally but then infuses his reading of passages with ironic incredulity. This performance undermines any monologic interpretation.

He begins at the beginning, reading:

> "In the beginning God created the heaven and the earth." It doesn't go into detail. He doesn't need to explain to you, you probably wouldn't understand it, because he's got a massive brain, and yours is little. Trust him, I did.

Gervais's stage persona deftly shifts between channeling this believer who "trusts" God but through his performance deconstructs Biblical literalism. Gervais's routine has all of the qualities mentioned so far. It is based on his active participation in the New Atheist zeitgeist of post-September 11 culture wars. He exposes monologic tendencies (in this case, biblical literalism) and Bergsonian mechanical thinking. It is a charged comment meant to address serious social issues, designed to earn the comedian a laugh.

3 Religious Satire and Doubting Thomases

"I'm Here Promoting – Doubt"

Faith accepts claims while skepticism demands proof. Many humorists have explored this realm of incredulity, questioning both the nature of religious thought and the existence of God. While religious dogma is often steeped in monologic discourse, comedians critique and lampoon such religious certainty. These comedians sometimes seem to adopt what I have identified as a Doubting Thomas role, reacting to supernatural or pseudoscientific utterances with exaggerated skepticism. Satire musters a certain zeal to question. Meanwhile, the parody of any faith or dogma represents a dialogic take on the nature of and indeed the location of God in contemporary culture. Taken together, this zeal to doubt is a cornerstone to religious humor.

> If there was a God, don't you think he'd have flicked Hitler's head off?
> – Eddie Izzard

In traditional theological debates, the various challenges presented by the fact of suffering to faith is categorized as theodicy. In *Philosophy of Religion*, Louis P. Pojman summarizes the central issue as "The problem of evil arises from the paradox of an omnibenevolent, omnipotent deity's allowing the existence of evil" (151). Theodicy is not inherently an issue of atheism, per se, rather it is a paradox the faithful must grapple with.

> Why didn't he create a better world, if not one without evil, at least one with substantially less evil than this world? Many have contended that this paradox ... is not just a paradox but an implicit contradiction.
> (Pojman 151)

Bart Ehrman added this explanation of theodicy's etymology:

> The term is made up of two Greek words: theos, which means "God." And "diké," which means "justice." Theodicy, in other words, refers to the problem of how God can be "just" or "righteous" given the fact that

there is so much suffering in the world he allegedly created and is sovereign over.

(*God's Problem* 8)

J. H. Charlesworth puts it concisely, "How can God allow such evils? How can the one almighty God allow his select people to suffer such horrors?" ("Theodicy in Early Jewish Writings," 484 in *Theodicy in the World of the Bible* edited by Antti Laato and Johannes C. de Moor).

Raphael Lataster summarized the theological struggle with evil this way:

> [T]heists cannot really move the goalposts much on God's omnipotence and omniscience, there seems to me to always be sufficient wriggle room to raise objections about what God's omnibenevolence really entails; what "good" actually is; what "evil" actually is . . . and what can be considered reasonable prevention requirements, trade-offs, rights, justifications, and rationale, even if that results in significant concessions or explanations that need not be probable, merely possible.
>
> ("The Argument from Evil, the Argument from Hiddenness, and Supernaturalistic Alternatives to Theism" 938)

In other words, any hypothetical supernatural deity has no obligation to be good in any sense we-who-postulate-their-existence understand. Therefore, theodicy never really works well to settle the "does God exist?" question. But it does highly problematize the notion of a "good" deity as humans generally understand the word.

One famous example of a believer struggling with this contradiction is Mother Teresa's letter to "a spiritual confidant, the Rev. Michael van der Peet" expressing her concern over a God who would let the poor suffer. She wrote, "I am told God loves me – and yet the reality of darkness & coldness & emptiness is so great that nothing touches my soul. Did I make a mistake in surrendering blindly to the Call of the Sacred Heart?" (http://time.com/4126238/mother-teresas-crisis-of-faith/).

All of the well-known authors and thinkers associated with the New Atheism movement have raised theodicy. For example, in *Letter to a Christian Nation*, Sam Harris summarizes it thus,

> people of faith regularly assure one another that God is not responsible for human suffering. But how else can we understand that God is both omniscient and omnipotent? This is the age-old problem of theodicy, and we should consider it solved. If God exists, either He can do nothing to stop the most egregious calamities, or He does not care to. God, therefore, is either impotent or evil.

(55)

Some of the humorists in this study have also explored the question of theodicy. For example, humorist and also outspoken humanist Stephen Fry, when asked in an interview what he would ask God if suddenly confronted by Him in the afterlife, responded "Bone cancer in children? What's that about?" (www.youtube.com/watch?v=2-d4otHE-YI). However, the problem of evil or suffering is not considered a strong argument against there being supernatural deities, as such. In Richard Dawkins's book *The God Delusion*, while critiquing what he calls the "God hypothesis," he notes that suffering itself is "an argument only against the existence of a Good God. Goodness is no part of the *definition* of the God Hypothesis, merely a desirable add-on" (135, his italics).

As a philosophical concern, theodicy tends to reside more in the debates of believers, such as in the Mother Teresa example. To further illustrate this element, Bart Ehrman cites his inquiries into suffering as the primary question that moved him from believer to nonbeliever. He explained:

> I realized that I could no longer reconcile the claims of faith with the facts of life. In particular, I could no longer explain how there can be a good and all-powerful God actively involved in this world, given the state of things. For many people who inhabit this planet, life is a cesspool of misery and suffering.
> (*God's Problem* 3)

Thus, the theological issue of theodicy is not limited to atheistic arguments. Indeed, what might be characterized as cruelty or indifference does not in and of itself make an argument pro or against the *prima facie* existence of deities. However, it does create a wedge issue that lends itself to the language games exercised by comedians. The problem of suffering in the world becomes an arena in which doubt may be exposed and exploited by satirizing it. The problem is universal, the doubt it engenders feels familiar, and comedians often seek universal themes while building their act. On the relative commonness of this type of doubt among believers, Ehrman explained, "But I do know that many thinking people think about suffering, this is in no small reason because all of us suffer." (*God's Problem* 18). For example, Eddie Izzard (in her 2009 comedy special *Stripped*) questioned, "If there was a God, don't you think he'd have flicked Hitler's head off?"

Pojman explains that "Western thought has distinguished between two types of evil: moral and natural" (152). So-called moral evils refer to suffering that is caused by humans. The horrors associated with Hitler would be an example, which Izzard deftly highlights in the joke above. In contrast, "Natural evil . . . includes those terrible events that occur in nature of their own accord, such as hurricanes, tornados, earthquakes" (Pojman 152). Atheist writer P. Z. Myers captures this aspect of theodicy when he introduces what he calls a joke, "Stop me if you've heard this one before" and then recounts a tale, in joke format, of a man with cancer receiving lifesaving medical treatments and when "his cancer goes into remission" proclaims "Praise Jesus! My prayers were answered!" (14). It seems, Myers observes, "No one seems to blame the omnipotent sky deity for causing the cancer in the first place.... God gets a lot of good press" (15). This is a contradiction that many humorists have lampooned. Both Marc Maron and Jim Jefferies have done routines on this theme.

Maron's 2002 comedy album *Not Sold Out* includes a routine where he describes his agent using the events of September 11 as a reason for Maron to move from New York City to Los Angeles. This is 2002, and September 11 is still a very raw topic. He then explains how he responded:

> You got earthquakes in LA. Our city may be the target of terrorism, but yours is the target of God. And God, of course, arguably the greatest terrorist of all time. He's going to get everybody for no reason at all. "Why did he have to die?" "God decided it was his time."
> What a fucking asshole.

The all-too-human lament "Why did he have to die?" is in the realm of theodicy, and Maron uses it to emphasize that any God who would allow suffering, indeed be the cause of suffering, must be an "asshole." Though Izzard never goes as far as calling God an "asshole" for allowing Hitler, it is philosophically the same point.

> Religious people will forgive God for fuckin' anything. In their mind he does good things, rainbows, children's laughter, shit like that, right?
> – Jim Jefferies (*I Swear to God* 2009)

With his brash, Australian stage persona, however, Jim Jefferies takes this same theme and goes even further. On his 2009 HBO special *I Swear to God*, he also confronts the habit of some religious people to excuse God's cruel ways as mysterious and unknowable. He says, "religious people will forgive God for fuckin' anything. In their mind he does good things, rainbows, children's laughter, shit like that, right?" Then, Jefferies turns to the issues of theodicy, raising a litany of natural and moral evils: "When He does bad things like hurricanes, AIDS, cancer, child molestation, then they just go, 'Oh, well. God works in mysterious ways.' What type of an excuse is that? What is mysterious about acting like a fucking asshole?" Jefferies lampoons this readiness to excuse by extending it into an outrageously extreme suggestion:

> If I ever date a religious girl she's gonna come home and I'm gonna be raping her mum. Right? And she's gonna look at me and go, "What are you doing?" And I'm gonna go, "I'm mysterious. I've always been mysterious."

Evoking this excuse in the face of one of the most horrendous acts satirizes the thinness of the apologist position.

Both Maron and Jefferies use the epithet "asshole" to attach blame to the character of God. It also extends to the effect of showing dissonance and hypocrisy in the beliefs of followers. Also referring to ecological disasters, John Oliver and Andy Zaltzman do a routine together as part of Oliver's 2008 special *Terrifying Times*. Twice during this show, Oliver brings out a guest, his long-time co-host on the podcast *The Bugle*, who he introduces as The Professor of Fact at the University of Great Britain, Professor Andy Zaltzman. In this professorial character, sitting at a desk with a white lab coat on, Zaltzman displays his style of wit and wordplay, turning every question upside-down with irony and unexpected comedic turns. Instead of "asshole," they compare God's natural evils to the behavior of an old, out-of-date racist. Zaltzman opines, "if this is the way the big man works, then looking at where he sends these natural disasters, then God is clearly a racist. And quite a naughty racist as well. He clearly hates Africa." He continues:

> Of course, God's friends and supporters would spring to his defense and say, "Well, he's just from a different generation. You know, you gotta understand, he doesn't really understand the issues, and sometimes he doesn't even realize he's being racist. Different times, different values." Say what you like about God, depending on where you live, of course, but he is bad role model for our youth.
>
> Religious people are in the crowd, and they don't like hearing facts.
> – Jim Jefferies

In *I Swear to God*, Jefferies jokes about pedophiles in the Catholic Church, and when some members of the audience groan, he responds. He claims that those who groan are religious people and, "they don't like hearing facts." Confronting religious people with facts as a way to raise questions about the nature of faith is another rhetorical strategy adopted by comedians that emerges, playing the role of a Doubting Thomas. The comedian known as Earthquake had a very clear and concrete example of faithless hypocrisy in his season 7 episode 5 *Comedy Central Presents*, when he quipped, "The Pope went to St. Louis in a bullet-proof limo. I like 'Damn, where's his faith!'" (2003).

Human suffering amid both human evil and natural disasters is associated with a rise in atheism. In *Defending God*, James L. Crenshaw summarizes this thought "For many Westerners today, the natural response to the evils that beset us is to deny the existence of God" (25). Crenshaw continues, "for the twentieth century, catalysts included the gas chambers at Dachau and Treblinka and the atomic bombs dropped on Hiroshima and Nagasaki. After these horrors, any talk about a providential ruler of the universe rings hallow" (25). Our twenty-first century catalyst was the terrorist attacks on September 11, 2001. New Atheism clearly stands as a reactionary force to the horrors of that event. And on a parallel philosophical course, some comedians echoed the hollowness of a divine hand by lampooning the paradox between a loving God and the suffering of people.

The "Doubting Thomas" character type appears in the story of Doubting Thomas found in the Gospel of John (20:24–29). In it, the disciple known of Thomas doubted that the other disciples had seen the resurrected Jesus.

> "But he said unto them, Except I shall see in his hands the print of the nails, and put my finger into the print of the nails, and thrust my hand into his side, I will not believe." Jesus came to him and let Thomas examine and also touch his wounds, and with that proof Thomas accepted Jesus's divinity and resurrection.

In his book *Doubting Thomas*, Glenn W. Most examines this character type in literature and art. Most notes "in the narrative John has devised, Thomas above all plays the role of doubter." Most explains that "doubt" is etymologically related to "two," which he interprets as meaning that "doubt is being conceived above all as the response to a situation in which there are two alternatives, of which it is not certain which is the right one" (*Doubting Thomas* 80).

This process of demonstrating alternatives but without certainty about either, as suggested by Most, resonates with Northrop Frye's study of satire. Frye indicates that the satirist's role is not necessarily to be right per se. Rather, it is to point out moments in society when public figures or institutions fail in their responsibilities to society. According to Frye, satire represents a "struggle of two societies, one normal and the other absurd" (224).

Comedy contains many examples of doubt being used in satire. Incredulity of religious accounts of miracles as well as other religious themes in the modern world is a ubiquitous rhetorical strategy utilized by comedians and humorists. Some instances may take the form of doubting the existence of God, and another variant is questioning the presence of evil in the world. One striking example of the role of rhetorical doubt is particularly essential to the themes and structure of the Bill Maher film *Religulous*. In this film, Maher casts himself as a purveyor of doubt.

In a piece for *Esquire* titled "Comedians as Prophets," Scott Raab observed of comics, "They aren't seers or priests. They are teachers." If so, in *Religulous* what is Maher "teaching"? Early in the film, he sets out his agnostic lesson plan: "that's what I'm here promoting – doubt. That's my product. . . . The other guys are selling certainty, not me. I'm on the corner with doubt." Like the biblical Doubting Thomas who is said to have spread the Gospel in foreign lands evangelizing, the film is also a travelogue, as Maher travels the globe engaging with believers and leaders about their belief systems, teaching doubt in every case. Raab further describes comedians as "Takers of liberties, givers of offense, their hostility is deliberate, their cruelty relentless – freeing us to laugh at our weakness, pain, and rage. No wonder we repay them with love."

Religulous and the Performance of Doubt

Stop with the faith, start with the doubt.

– Bill Maher

In a Larry King interview from 2007 discussing the forthcoming film *Religulous* (later released in 2008), King asked if the film represented an atheist view, and Maher answered "It is certainly the doubter's view." He then adds, "Stop with the faith, start with the doubt." By casting himself as a doubter in the film, Maher assumes the role of a Doubting Thomas. For example, early in the film, Maher visits a Trucker's Chapel in Rayleigh, North Carolina. The small congregation gives Maher the podium, and he asks them, "Are you ever bothered by many things that are in Christianity that are not in the Bible?" The group discusses this for a moment, with Maher playing the part of the Doubting Thomas, poking and prodding at their answers. He finally asks them, "Why is faith good? Why is believing something without evidence good?" Eventually one of the congregants marches off in the middle of the scene, declaring "You start disputing my God, and you got a problem. I don't know what you – I'm outta here. You do what you wanna do, but I'm outta here."

The Apostle Thomas is also known as Didymus which means "the twin" which furthers this theme of ambivalency between two possible versions of reality. Frye's aforementioned struggle between normalcy and absurdity is embodied by Maher here, as he becomes a "twin" of sorts. Maher mirrors back biblical and dogmatic notions, lampooning by showing the absurdity directly back in his encounters.

Steven Weisenburger offers an approach to satire in the context of postmodern literature. Weisenburger critiques Frye's approach, "Satire in this generative mode does not participate in the oppositional" ("Fables of Subversion" 2). Weisenburger suggests that satire can be subversive. "I have sought to define a tradition of American satirical writings that realize the subversive potential of the form" which he goes on to describe as "firebombing the cultural theater where meanings are made" (259–261).

Satire as an oppositional act of firebombing suits to describe Maher's aggressive approach to religious satire. In *Religulous*, he generally avoids actively mocking believers through this performance of a mirror. His twinning as it were attempts to make his interlocutors uncomfortable with their own assumptions. His posture is one of spreading doubt. This doubt turns out to be just as much of a firebomb. *Religulous* contains many examples of this rhetorical posture of doubt being used as satire and Maher's performance of doubt is particularly essential. Incredulity of religious accounts of miracles as well as other religious themes in the modern world is a ubiquitous rhetorical strategy utilized by comedians and humorists.

Prophecy and Frankness

As in Raab's piece, other commentators have noted over the past few years that comedians function as truth-sayers who speak back to power and are public intellectuals. Megan Garber expresses this point thus, "Comedians have taken on the role of public intellectuals. They're exploring and wrestling with important ideas."

As part of a series of lectures in 1983, Michel Foucault explained the classical Greek concept of *parrhesia*. Foucault's speeches have been gathered together in an edited version, *Discourse and Truth: the Problematization of Parrhesia* (edited by Joseph Pearson. Digital Archive: Foucault.info, 1999. <https://foucault.info/parrhesia/about/> accessed December 27, 2019). Foucault defines *parrhesia* as "to say everything" that is on one's mind and, among other qualities, emphasizes the importance of frankness.

> The one who uses parrhesia, the parrhesiastes, is someone who says everything he has in mind: he does not hide anything, but opens his heart and mind completely to other people through his discourse. In parrhesia, the speaker is supposed to give a complete and exact account of what he has in mind so that the audience is able to comprehend exactly what the speaker thinks.
> (2 https://foucault.info/parrhesia/)

In his introduction to a special issue of *Studies in American Humor* 5.1, James Caron also mentions the central role *parrhesia* occupies, claiming "satire today stubbornly propagates its comic parrhesia, its inherent intent to speak truth to power, an effort I call 'truthiness satire' to acknowledge how it operates now as a comic supplement to the postmodern sphere" (7). Chris A. Kramer emphasizes another important aspect of the speaker of such frankness, the "parrhesiastes" must not only be bold and free with their words, but additionally, the speaker must be coming from a position of lower power than the social force being criticized ("Parrehisa, Humor, and Resistance." *The Israeli Journal of Humor Research* June 2020: 24). As Foucault put it, they must be "less powerful than the one with whom he or she speaks. The parrhesia comes from 'below' as it were, and is directed towards 'above'" (Foucault 1983: 4–5). As applied in the context of comedy, Kramer notes:

> This form of humor is inextricably linked to their parrhesiastic truth-telling. . . . Their humorous, playful attitude offers a form of seeing reality that is more incisive and accurate than the modes of perceiving predominantly found in the serious, epistemically closed, rule-following people on positions of power.
> (43)

Foucault contrast parrhesia with rhetoric, which is practiced speech designed to manipulate. Foucault claimed, "In Seneca, for example, one finds the idea that personal conversations are the best vehicle for frank speaking and truth-telling insofar as one can dispense, in such conversations, with the need for rhetorical devices and ornamentation." This contrast between personal conversation and rhetorical devices is evident in the stylistic circumstance of stand-up comedy. Certainly, stand-up comedy *is*, of course, a practiced rhetorical style, but the aesthetic posture of most stand-up is to strive for a conversational tone and intimacy, thus allowing it to incorporate a veneer of frankness. Ironically, the apparent lack of rhetoric is the rhetorical posture of most stand-up comedy.

Bill Maher, in any case, has always insisted on the importance of frankness. He has on numerous occasions expressed the belief that his viewers seem to respect his honesty. Maher thinks that for what he does to be effective, viewers and his fans have to believe he is sincere. In a 1999 interview with *Rolling Stone* magazine, he explained:

> the people are there for this show. I think they sense the honesty. That's what Politically Incorrect means – it means I'm not bullshitting. ABC just did a focus group last year – only fourteen percent of the people said they agree with me most of the time, yet they still like the show, because people respect honesty.

Maher claims to never take iconoclastic positions simply to create controversy but because he himself is personally invested in them. He put it another way in a 2011 interview with Tim Dickinson when he claimed, "The American people don't care what side of an issue you're on. . . . They just don't want you to act like a pussy."

Trying to apply the notion of risk to stand-up comedy is also a paradoxical one, since professional comedians make their living speaking out, so comedians such as Maher, Bill Hicks, George Carlin, Richard Pryor, and others found that when they took risks they also gained professionally and financially. Naturally, counterexamples exist, instances when controversial comments have caused some performers to experience professional or financial setbacks. Maher's career suffered when ABC canceled *Politically Incorrect* in 2002 after his post-9/11 comment, "We have been the cowards, lobbing cruise missiles from 2,000 miles away. That's cowardly. Staying in the airplane when it hits the building, say what you want about it, [it's] not cowardly." Ironically, the very same week his show was canceled, Maher received the LA Press Club's President's Award for his championing of free speech.

Multivariant Realities Interviewing Actor-Jesus at the Holy Land Experience Theme Park

Another section of the film *Religulous* highlights Maher's visit to The Holy Land Experience, a Christian theme park in Orlando, Florida. This contemporary and tourist-oriented experience perfectly exemplifies Jean Baudrillard's critique of hyperreality. The park's website describes its goal as:

> It is a living, biblical museum that takes you 7000 miles away and 2000 years back in time to the land of the Bible. Its combination of sights, sounds, and tastes will stimulate your senses and blend together to create a spectacular new experience. . . . But above all, beyond the fun and excitement, we hope that you will see God and His Word exalted and that you will be encouraged in your search for enduring truth and the ultimate meaning of life.
>
> (<www.holylandexperience.com/> accessed March 12, 2017)

This thoroughly self-proclaimed literal interpretation of the Bible results in a fantasy environment. It is not in any fashion the "authentic" story of "the land of the Bible," but a Baudrillardian fourth order simulation: "it has no relation to any reality whatsoever, it is its own pure simulacrum" (6). It embodies the hyperreal, "the generation of the real without origin or reality" (1). By recreating not only a religious mythology but also a re-interpreted religious dogma, the park no longer even refers to its own traditional scripture. This is clearly the postmodern hyperreal due to the irony of their creationist claim to biblical authority. Baudrillard describes religion in general as, "no longer itself anything but a gigantic simulacrum-not unreal, but a simulacrum, that is to say, never exchanged for the real, but exchanged for itself, an uninterrupted circuit without reference" (6). Simply showing some of the events at the park, including a recreation of the crucifixion and dancing Israelites, communicates the incongruous, nonliteral fake "literalness" of the park. Maher also interviews park employees and park visitors. For example, as part of his agenda of spreading doubt, he challenges a group of visitors if they really believe that the story of Noah's ark is plausible.

The more remarkable scene, however, is when Maher interviews an unnamed actor who plays the role of Jesus at the park. Actors in all situations occupy multivariant states whereby the audience's brain recognizes them as both themselves and their respective character. This duck-rabbit feature of both jokes and acting is on display in this segment. How are we the audience to judge this interaction? We see a figure clad in the attire of a Jesus, but we know he is an actor and not *the* "Jesus." At times, this ambiguity adds to the humor, but it also adds to creating an odd interview. This feature is relevant as Maher himself shifts between both realities. He is both trying to interview the actor and also trying to interview a proxy Jesus. Maher acknowledges the fakeness of everything around them when he points to a round rock outside the replica tomb and asks the actor-Jesus "Is this a real rock?" And actor-Jesus plays his role of actor/park representative by simply explaining that it is not real, but "more of a visual."

Maher then turns his attention to the actor-Jesus with a humorous quip that embodies the tension of the multivariant image, saying "I've seen you around." The actor-Jesus replies with aplomb that Maher himself must often get recognized in public. But when Maher turns to theology (and his agenda of doubt), he tries to force the actor-Jesus to become a stable character, as a proxy for Jesus. Maher's segue reveals the difficulty of this move, as he says "Let me ask you some questions about your business, well really, the Jesus business." He then asks the actor-Jesus about the existence of evil in the world (aka theodicy), and why would God allow the devil to even exist. However, since the actor-Jesus is NOT the Jesus but an actor-playing-Jesus, theodicy is not the actor-Jesus's business (theater is this young man's business!). The actor does try to supply some answers, but he is clearly no theologian and makes no cogent replies.

Unsettled movements of meaning – is Maher a comedian or a journalist, is the actor Jesus or a performer, is the whole theme part a ministry or an entertainment – create fertile possibilities for the satirist. But some commentators find having things so unsettled unsettling. Robert N. Spicer raises this line of questioning in his article, "Before and After *The Daily Show*: Freedom and Consequences in Political satire." Spicer wonders what sort of consequences Jon Stewart and Stephen Colbert might face, sensing perhaps that they comport themselves as immune to consequences. Spicer wonders aloud, "As with the satirists who preceded him, Jon Stewart is faced with the unintended consequences of his actions" (38). Frankly, I am not sure what these unintended consequences Spicer muses about are, nor am I sure why he suggests that Stewart or any other comedian must face them. Spicer suggests that comedians use their status as comedians as a shield, but in fact they *are comedians* and as noted elsewhere their first call to action is chasing a laugh. One is not sure what else Spicer expects.

In *Religulous*, before either Maher or the actor-Jesus can get too far with this interview, they are interrupted by an unnamed park employee who identifies herself as the Senior Manager of Public Relations. She shuts the interview down and complains that she was not properly informed about who would be doing the interview. She is unhappy with Maher's presence, and explains that this is because "of what he is and because of the types of show (sic) that he does." She is, one supposes, not wrong, either. After all, on an episode of *Real Time* from October 2011, Maher described all religion as a con job, saying "Religion itself is a con, and it's a con you pull on your own mind." That is probably not the image the park expected when they first agreed to allow filming.

Northrop Frye suggests that the satirist's primary job is to point out the immorality or hypocrisy of a ruling class (political, religious, et al). Frye called satire "inconvenient truth." This is Raab's prophet and teacher. This is Foucault's brave speech and Garber's public intellectual. Garber explains,

"Humor has a moral purpose. Humor has intellectual heft." This is the Doubting Thomas described by Most. Thus, Doubting Thomas epitomizes both Maher's character in *Religulous* and his iconoclastic brand of satire. As Maher said in his 2011 *Rolling Stone* interview, "Free speech is alive and well in this country. You just have to fight for it."

4 Acting Out the Character of God

"Ridiculing the Incarnation"

> Made you a planet.
> I can't breathe.
> Would you like an atmosphere?
> – Ricky Gervais
> *Out of England 2* (2010)

In the above bit, Gervais deftly identifies the inherent paradox of an all-powerful and loving God with the rhetorical flourish that the Bible presents of His creating the Earth and Sky. In Genesis 1:7, the story goes that "God made the firmament, and divided the waters which were under the firmament from the waters which were above the firmament." Gervais revisits this biblical tale in his deconstruction of the children's story book *Noah and the Ark* that Gervais holds up for ridicule in his 2010 HBO special *Out of England 2* (a version of this routine can also be found on his 2009 comedy special *Science*). As satire, it is biting and to the point. Rhetorically, how does Gervais structure and create this humor?

Playing to large venues, the reading of this book (and it is a real book!) includes projections of each page so that the audience can see what he is responding to. In this way, the entire routine is built on the basic joke structure discussed earlier of observing something and then reacting to what you observed, with the reaction constituting the punch line, the funny part so to speak. His reaction to each page contains many of the satiric rhetorical devices discussed thus far. Using *reducto ad absurdum*, he lampoons the Bible story by reacting dialogically to it, identifying multivariate meanings in the book's monologic dogma.

In the joke cited above, by having God ask if humans would "Like an atmosphere?" he visits the topic of theodicy, which is an essential part of the Noah and the Ark story as depicted in Genesis 6–7. In it, it is God who chooses to wipe out all humans as a punishment, which Gervais identifies as "genocide." Furthermore, given the general unlikelihood of such a global flood, the routine also allows Gervais to play the character of a scientifically minded Doubting Thomas. Furthermore, his interrogation of a children's book version of the Bible story is reminiscent of Maher's interview with an actor portraying Jesus, as both are multivariant proxies for what they represent (such children's books of Bible tales are another example of Baudrillard's fourth-order simulacrum).

This particular joke also introduces another rhetorical device, which shall be the topic of this chapter, the "act out." As a comedy bit being performed by a stand-up comedian, Gervais is doing an "act out." In this type of joke, the comedian sets up the joke as per normal, with an observation about the world, but instead of a common dialogue-based punch line, he or she actually acts out their own suggestion. An act out is whenever a comedian makes a suggestion and then presents the suggestion to their audience, *in situ* as it were. In the case of this joke, Gervais acts out both the character of God and humans in the story.

In her comedy guide *The Comedy Bible* (2001), Judy Carter defines the act out, "Instead of *talking about* someone or something, you *perform* it. You turn into the people or things you mentioned in the set up-actually act them out" (85, her italics). For example, in a routine presented before episode 3.2 of *Seinfeld*, Jerry Seinfeld performs a bit about extra buttons. He asks, "What kind a sicko would save these?" and then acts out someone going through a tiny file cabinet full of extra buttons. As the "sicko" character, he asks "Where the Hell is" and pretends to be going through a drawer searching for them. This is an example of an act out: Seinfeld's premise is asking "Who is the Sicko?" and the punch line is him acting like the sicko.

When one becomes aware of the technique, one begins to recognize how common it is. A very theatrical comedian, like Robin Williams, Eddie Izzard, or Dane Cook, clearly does numerous act outs, but so do many others. In fact, though often criticized for being a poor actor, Jerry Seinfeld's comedy is full of them. Just to present another example, Seinfeld has a joke where he asks out loud, "You give me an explanation as to why the pharmacist has to be two feet up, above everybody else" (*Seinfeld* Episode 3.10). A moment later, Seinfeld acts like a customer handing in his prescription, but to an unseen pharmacist that is clearly much higher. Reaching his arm way up and using a timid voice, he asks, in character, "I'd like to get this prescription" This pretending to be the sicko, to be the customer, doing what was just suggested, acting it out, is what comedians mean by an act out.

Another example of an act out being utilized in the context of religious satire can be found in Eddie Izzard's 2002 concert *Circle*. Having studied mime and clowning, as well as acting, Izzard (in a manner reminiscent of Robin Williams) is known for her act outs and a good deal of her stand-up is based on act outs. Just to give one other example, in her breakthrough special *Dressed to Kill* (1999), Izzard does an act out based on the premise that whoever invented the Heimlich Maneuver must have used trial and error: "He must have experimented, he was organized, he was German." This observation is followed by a hilarious act out in which she (using a German accent in the persona of Dr. Heimlich) tries different actions leading up to the discovery of the now eponymous maneuver. "Okay maybe this, bam, okay now maybe with a frying pan POW! Must be a combination" and so on. Every portion is shown by Izzard doing the action, which culminates in a cacophony of sound effects, accents, and proto-Heimlich maneuvers. This is Izzard acting out the development of the Heimlich Maneuver.

To return to *Circle*, the entire show has lengthy bits on religion. Izzard never expressly addresses September 11, but clearly this show was developed in this time frame and reflects the concerns I am investigating. In *Circle*, Izzard does a lengthy and hilarious act out of Jesus trying to preach his Father's gospel to dinosaurs. In this written format, I will never capture the full impact of Izzard's performance, but here is a transcript of the routine taken from the special (with stage directions added by me):

> But then Jesus had to go down onto the planet earth and preach the word of the lord to the dinosaurs.... And he goes to the world, and there's dinosaurs everywhere. "Roar, growl, (dinosaur gibberish noises)" said Jesus, trying to blend in. And he goes into a dinosaur bar. (act out as if pushing open Western-style saloon doors.) As soon as he walks in, all the dinosaurs stop what they're doing. (act out a dinosaur piano player who stops mid-song and stares.) Other dinosaurs playing cards (act out a dinosaur dealing some cards, then stops and stares. The card-playing dinosaur checks his cards while eyeing Jesus.) "Rawr," says the card-playing dinosaur. Jesus said "My name is Jesus, and I'm son of god . . . in one religion. I've come to read you the stuff from my father's book, that we're hoping to get a publisher for. It's called the Holy Bib-lee" (Izzard mispronounces the word intentionally) "we may change the pronunciation on that.... Anyway, these are just some ideas, you know, these are all rough. One is, "blessed are the meek for they shall inherit the earth." "Rawr," responds one dinosaur. (as Jesus again) "Alright, we'll cross that one out." . . . "What about, blessed are the huge scaly monsters, for they shall doubtlessly inherit the earth, unless something awful happens with the temperature."

Izzard represents an interesting case study in my research. Although arguably not as didactic as Bill Maher, she clearly shares a similar spirit and intentionality. Like Maher, Izzard became increasingly interested in religious satire, the power of secular thought as well as politics, after September 11. In 2013, she received the Outstanding Lifetime Achievement Award in Cultural Humanism presented by Harvard's Humanist Community. The event was covered in "Izzard accepts humanist award" by Zohra D. Yaqhubi (*The Harvard Crimson* February 21, 2013). As reported, in her acceptance speech, she remarked, "Science is full of theories. Religion is just full of stories. . . .

They're stories, in which case Lord of the Rings is the same." Izzard questioned the religious figures present in many faiths, taking issue with the notion of a God figure who demands human sacrifice and constant praise but does not make an appearance in times of extreme suffering.

An interviewer asked Izzard, "George Carlin once said that the role of the comedian is to find where the line is drawn and then cross it. In your mind, what is the role?" In her answer, Izzard directly addresses religious satire, saying:

> I was reading about that and saw it was the Golden Rule, and it's in Christianity, and it's in Judaism, and it's in Islam, and it's in Hindu faith. It's in all of them, fucking hell. That's not crossing the line, that's just saying treat other people as you'd like to be treated yourself. I think that's the only thing in religion you need. You don't need the prayers, the fig, the body of Christ, the thing with the hammer – any of that shit, forget it all. Just treat people as you'd like to be treated. Now that gets rid of a whole load of religious paraphernalia, but I think it's true. That's all you bloody need.

With examples such as Gervais, Seinfeld, and Izzard, I have been trying to explain the concept of the act out. To summarize, I have come to identify this use of act outs to give voice to religious figures or deities as a common rhetorical strategy utilized by some comedians who do religious satire. Rhetorically, this is an important observation. On review, one discovers that acting out a god, or *the* God, or Jesus, or some other deity, is a common tool of religious satire. I initially introduced act outs with the phrase "ridiculing the incarnate" an invective first hurled at the 1979 Monty Python film *The Life of Brian*. A good deal of controversy surrounded the film, which depicted the fictional and marginal accidental messiah Brian, who stumbles his way haplessly through a life that seems to mirror some of the things normally associated with the Life of Jesus, including a "virginal" (actually "not-so-virginal") mother and crucifixion. Some religious people and communities were offended, considering the whole film as disrespectful toward the figure of Jesus.

In 1979, it was the subject of a debate presented on British television. On November 9, 1979, the BBC2 television program *Friday Night, Saturday Morning* hosted a debate between John Cleese and Michael Palin of Monty Python and two religious apologists on the question of whether or not *The Life of Brian* was disrespectful to religion. During the discussion, noted religious conservative Malcolm Muggeridge time and time again described the film's lampooning of the Messiah-figure as both offensive and misleading, not to mention immature and too-easy comedy. Muggeridge insisted repeatedly that the film was a "ridiculing of . . . the Incarnation, in an extremely cheap and tenth-rate way." Though the members of the Python troupe denied that they were either ridiculing or even depicting the historical Jesus Christ, some still found Monty Python's depiction of Brian-as-stand-in-for-Christ offensive.

Acting Out the Character of God 41

The Life of Brian depicts the life of the decidedly "not the messiah" Brian, portrayed by Graham Chapman. Brian's life oddly parallels the life of Jesus, even being born in a manger across the road from Jesus. This causes the three wise men to accidentally give their gifts to baby Brian and then to take them back again so that they can deliver them to the baby Jesus. Besides establishing in the first scene that baby Brian was not meant to be taken as the literal baby Jesus, the scene also foreshadowed actual religious leaders mistaking the film's messiah for the one found in the New Testament. And so it goes, up to and including Brian's eventual crucifixion. The Pythons repeatedly stated at the time and since that the film clearly was not about Jesus, but that hasn't stopped some religious-minded people from being offended by the film. It was the subject of protests and boycotts, some as recently as 2013.

Inspired by Malcolm Muggeridge's apparent obsession that the Pythons were "ridiculing the Incarnate," I have imported the phrase and am willfully misusing it to capture the essence of the comedic act out as a rhetorical device specifically for lampooning religious figures and ideas. "Ridiculing the incarnate" seems an apt phrase to dissect here. In the original context, Muggeridge used it to disparage satiric depictions of Jesus. But going forward, I intend to appropriate the phrase ironically, meaning the rhetorical strategy by comedians and humorists to act out a deity as a way to admonish hypocrites or underscore logical fallacies, to put "inconvenient truths" into the mouths of godly figures. Satiric act outs of religious personages are also included under this coinage.

> I gave this to you, mother fucker, are you crazy? The polar bears are brown. What did you do to the polar bears?
>
> – Louis C.K.

Acting out the voice of Jesus et al. gives comedians a chance to tackle a host of social issues. Three common topics have been regularly satirized by this method. One can find many comedians using the voice of god to critique political pundits who use religion as a justification for their positions, the Bible itself (including satirizing biblical literalism), and to question the role of suffering in the world (theodicy, as described in Chapter 3). And examples that come post September 11 operate in the cultural milieu that includes the New Atheists.

For example, in August 2013, Rush Limbaugh used "belief in god" to justify climate change denial, saying, "If you believe in God, then intellectually you cannot believe in manmade global warming. You must be either agnostic or atheistic to believe that man controls something he can't create." Contrast Limbaugh's remarks with an act out Louis C.K. did in 2011 that embodies the counterpoint:

> Some people are environmentalists and some people are what whatever the opposite of environmentalist is, and like whatever they think

that they're slowing down the economy creating restrictions. . . . But a lot of these people are Christians, a lot of these people are very devout Christians and that's such a confusing thing to me that if you believe that god gave you the earth, that god created the earth for you, why would you not have to look after it? Why would not think that when He came back He would go "What the fuck did you do? I gave this to you, mother fucker, are you crazy? The polar bears are brown. What did you do to the polar bears? Did you shit all over every polar bear? Who spilled this shit, who spilled this? Come over – did you fucking spill this?"

(*Live at the Beacon Theatre* 2011)

This routine exemplifies the satiric act of lampooning. As noted above, Greek satire consisted of lampooning, that is, taking the notions of others and exaggerating them in a form of *reducto ad absurdum*. In the usual logic of debate, *reducto ad absurdum* is considered a fallacy. In logic, it involves the misrepresentation of your opponent's position by presenting an unfair and perverted version of it. But, in the logic of comedy, presenting an unfairly perverted version of an idea becomes a way to critique it. The comedian takes the original point and rides it like a toboggan down the slippery slope of illogic until reaching the very bottom – a version so ridiculous that the original suggestion becomes exposed as well. In the case of this Louis C.K. routine, he is lampooning the potential contradiction between believing "that god gave you the earth" but then refusing to "to look after it." The satiric point is created by then acting out the character of God discovering the earth in a spoiled state and being very angry about it! In the voice of God, Louis C.K. bellows, "Come over – did you fucking spill this?"

As noted earlier, in examples involving Marc Maron, satire is often considered conservative, and there is an inherent irony in comedians acting out Jesus, et al. After all, Maron, Izzard, Maher, Louis C.K., the Pythons, and other comedians do not typically ridicule Jesus, Mohammed, *per se* but instead give voice to comedic interpretations of such figures as a means to call out hypocrisy, logical inconsistencies, and hypocrisy. Muslim-American comedian Dean Obeidallah claimed that for him, there is no point in doing jokes about Mohammed. Instead,

> [i]t has nothing to do with religious beliefs. The reason, simply put, is that my comedy focuses on mocking the people in power; the ones who are committing the bad acts or holding elected office (and often those two are the same.) The Prophet Mohammed died nearly 1,500 years ago. He isn't doing anything. ISIS, al Qaeda and the like are, so they are the ones I will continue to mock.
>
> ("Is it OK for comedians to joke about religion?")

Written around the time of the terrorist attacks on the offices of Charlie Hebdo in Paris, in his essay "Is it OK for comedians to joke about religion?" Obeidellah describes the results of an informal survey of some comedians that he knows.

> So I asked about 20 comedians, via social media and email, about the Paris attack. Regardless of whether they were Muslims living in Cairo or atheists living in New York, the comics' responses were consistent: They denounced the Paris attack and stood up for freedom of expression. That was true even for some of the Muslim comedians.

He quotes some of the comics who responded, sharing for example the thoughts of

> Joe DeRosa (not a Muslim) mentioned, telling jokes about any religious figure, not just Mohammed, can be challenging. DeRosa said, "I've been physically threatened for telling Jesus jokes. . . . Am I a coward if I don't joke about certain things that could cause a dangerous reaction? Or am I smart? I honestly don't know."

Comedians sometimes use satiric tools to skewer leaders and followers, and their rigid dogma. And rather than just joke the incarnate, another distinct option includes that in some cases they might assume the character of the incarnate. By using the comedian device of the act out, it can be the voice of God that does the actual criticizing. This point is clear in both the Maron and the Louis C.K. examples.

Louis C.K. presents the inconvenient truth to climate deniers, who justify their position in religious terms (*a la* Limbaugh): Louis C.K.'s performance of their god is going to hold them accountable. Do they really think God is going to approve of them destroying the planet, or "shitting all over the polar bears"? Limbaugh seems to be suggesting that belief in God absolves one of responsibility for stewardship or the planet. The voice of God presented by Louis C.K. contradicts this assumption. He reminds believers that their own belief system demands that they shall be held responsibility for their actions but their own god they claim to believe in.

Also, by addressing the issue of climate change, Louis C.K. is also taking a pro-science and pro-environmental point of view. This emphasis on science and logic is a reoccurring theme in New Atheist-era religious satire. Louis C.K. is therefore also implying in this bit that if there is a God, then that God must also be pro-science. The god Louis C.K. is acting out presents an argument for siding with science on the issue of climate change. This is as much to say, if you believe in a God who created everything, then you must also believe in a god who created science. (This is covered more in Chapter 5.)

Parody Religions

> It is only cake! Oh my god! The only way sky cake tastes good is if up in the sky the sky cookie and sky pie people can't have the sky cake. That's the only way sky cake tastes good. (pause) I did not spend my life not raping and killing people to not go up in the sky and have cake. SKY CAKE!
>
> – Patton Oswalt

A similar strategy to voicing the incarnate is the presentation of parody religions for humorous effect. Voicing the Incarnate – be it Jesus, Mohammod, God, the Pope, or whomever – rests on putting words or actions into the mouths of these figures. A parody religion seeks to highlight the absurdity of one or another religious precepts or behaviors. It can be surprising difficult to identify a parody religion, especially out of context. From the skeptic's perspective, both are made up out of whole cloth. In a deleted scene found as a DVD extra for *Religulous*, Bill Maher said of making up a religion:

> It's just too easy to start a religion. All you have to do is: A. think up some really powerful stupid shit. Some stuff that is so idiotic and weird that a person who believes it will be proving that ultimate virtue of faith; B. throw in some entitlements like life after death, washing away sins and free dental or whatever; and, C. wait. Just wait. Just say your bullshit and stick to it. Believe me, if you do that, if you just say it, they will come.

Some comedians have another variation of religious satire that voices the incarnate, not by acting out deities but instead by ridiculing dogma or practices in the form of parody religions (or parody religious rituals). Some high-profile examples of this include John Oliver's faux megachurch Our Lady of Perpetual Exemption, the Church of the Flying Spaghetti Monster, Bill Maher's Unbaptism, John Safran's Atheist Door-knocking skit, and Patton Oswalt's "sky cake" routine.

The unstable, dialogic nature of religious utterances and the possibility of multivariant images which might reincorporate religiosity into humorous material allows for many instances of comedians creating parody religions or parody religious rituals.

> Parody seems to offer a perspective on the present and the past which allows an artist to speak to a discourse from WITHIN it, but without being totally recuperated by it. Parody appears to have become, for this reason, the mode of the marginalized, or those who are fighting marginalization by a dominant ideology.
>
> (Hutcheon 206)

A joking representation of a pretend religion allows the performer to critique the religious concept being parodied while standing inside of the religious ritual and acting it out. By enacting the privileged position of the religious dogma, the comedian creates a social space from which to defend those who would otherwise be marginalized by the practice in question. The parody religion is also found in classical drama. For example, Aristophanes's *Lysistrata* includes a scene where the protagonist Lysistrata humiliates an old magistrate by dressing him first in a woman's veil and then making him go through a fake funeral. In this and other examples, even Aristophanes used fake religion or ritual as a form of *reducto ad absurdum*.

In the post-September 11 era, one can find many examples of parody religions and rituals used to champion secular values by exposing the most ridiculous or hurtful aspects of some religious dogmas. David Chidester reports, "the Yahoo Groups devoted to 'parody religions' expanded from about 120 in mid-2001 to over 400 by mid 2002" (*Authentic Fakes* 192). Chidester makes no mention of September 11 and his only direct reference to satire is Jonathon Swift's Aeolians, Chidester's observations neatly fold into mine about the zeitgeist of the period.

Through comic exaggeration and forceful lampooning, examples of socially charged parody religions include John Oliver's faux megachurch Our Lady of Perpetual Exemption and John Safran's door-to-door atheism skit in *John Safran vs God* (2004). As an internet, and now cultural, phenomenon another famous parody religion is the Church of the Flying Spaghetti Monster. It is often simply called the FSM, and its adherents have adopted the name Pastaferians. The FSM made its first public appearance during the 2005 Kansas Board of Education's debates over evolution versus Creationism (aka Intelligent Design) in their classrooms. Satire about Creationism is the subject of Chapter 5, but for now let's summarize this public moment.

The FSM is apparently the brainchild of Bobby Henderson, who has produced the book *The Gospel of the Flying Spaghetti Monster* and also maintains the Church's website. In 2005, he sent the Kansas Board of Education a letter demanding equal time for the Flying Spaghetti Monster's inclusion in the classroom alongside evolution and Creationism. He received no reply, so later he posted the letter on the internet. Since 2005, the FSM has increasingly appeared in public forums. They are represented in parades. Pastaferians decorate their houses during the holidays with appropriate markers (often including pasta, pirates, and strippers). On their website, the FSM claims that all humans descended from Pirates and "No one knows what the afterlife really holds, but we are told FSM Heaven has a Beer Volcano and Stripper Factory." They also wear a particular religious headdress – a Colander. There have been many reported cases of Pastaferians demanding their right to wear their religious headdress for public purposes such as driver's license photos.

A January 3, 2014 article in the Observer in Dunkirk, NY reports a new city council member being sworn in wearing his Colander:

> A unique style of headwear was present during newly-seated Pomfret Town Council member Christopher Schaeffer's oath of office Thursday afternoon, but it wasn't intended to keep his head warm. Schaeffer wore a colander (a strainer typically used to drain water from spaghetti) while Town Clerk Allison Dispense administered the oath of office to him before the board's reorganizational meeting.
> When the OBSERVER asked afterward why he wore a colander on his head, Schaeffer said he was a minister with an even more unique organization – the Church of the Flying Spaghetti Monster.

The FSM website celebrated, "this may be the first openly Pastafarian sworn into office. For sure, the first to be sworn in wearing a colander" (more on the FSM in Chapter 5).

In "Laughing Matters: 'Parody Religions' and the Command to Compare," Joseph Laycock describes a case in which a Pastafarian in Austria insisted on wearing his religious headgear (again, a strainer) in his driver license photo. "Austria generally forbids citizens from wearing head-coverings while posing for their driver's license photo," Laycock explains, "but exceptions are sometimes granted on religious grounds, such as Muslim women wearing hijab" (21). What followed was a three-year legal battle in which the man, Nico Alm, demanded the same civil rights as religious persons. According to Laycock, this is an example of an important function of parody religions: comparison. "Through parody, invented religions challenge the frame of comparison and demand a focus on difference rather than sameness. . . . How is Pastafaranism different from Intelligent Design?" (25) For example, in Alm's case, "by demanding accommodations for his parody religion, Alm sought to demonstrate that religious accommodations are untenable" (25). Thus, muddying the waters on the very question of what *is* a religion, parody religions create a framework that demand comparison and debate. They are heartily Bakhtinian in challenging the monologic discourse of religions and of the legal protections granted religion.

Laycock also claims that "many of the new adherents to Henderson's parody religion were aligned with the New Atheist movement" (25). He specifically references Richard Dawkins, who gave support to the idea of the Church of the Flying Spaghetti Monster in *The God Delusion*. It has always been central to New Atheists that religion be treated like any other set of ideas, and thus be open to criticism, rational debate, and even ridicule.

Dawkins makes the point: the rational question is not whether one can prove that god does not exist, it is "whether his existence is probable" (77). In a description of how the logical concept of "burden of proof" works, Dawkins compares the likelihood of deities such as God, Jesus, and Yahweh to rhetorical inventions such as the Flying Spaghetti Monster or Bertrand Russel's invisible teapot. Dawkins explains that "the burden of proof rests with believers, not non-believers . . . the odds in favour of the teapot (spaghetti monster/Esemrelda and Keith/unicorns etc.) are not equal to odds against" (76). In an interview on my podcast, Michael Nugent, Chairperson of Atheist Ireland, put it this way, "You have rights, your ideas do not."

On his HBO show *Real Time*, Bill Maher is known for tackling a whole range of social and political issues with irreverence and gusto. Julie Webber described *Real Time* as "interesting because it can be seen as a kind of flashpoint over many of the extended cultural wars that took place over the past decade" (*The Cultural Set Up of Comedy* 44). Maher's cultural flashpoint includes a regular dose of religious satire, of course. For example, on February 3, 2012, comedian Bill Maher performed the world's first "unbaptism." He ritualistically reversed the then-recent posthumous baptism of atheist and scientist (and father-in-law to Mitt Romney) Edward Davies by the Church of Latter Day Saints.

Maher performed his "unbaptism" at the end of his show with a segment in which he began by reporting:

> In case you didn't hear, it was discovered last week that Edward Davies, Ann Romney's father – an enthusiastically anti-religious scientist who called organized faith "hogwash," was posthumously baptized in the Mormon tradition 14 months after he died. . . . They tried to do it sooner, but he wouldn't stop spinning in his grave.

Posthumous baptism is a Mormon ritual that goes back to 1840 and is often justified on the grounds of scriptural interpretations about the importance of baptism to enter heaven. However, many groups – both religious such as Orthodox Jews and secular such as atheists – find the practice offensive.

In addition to Maher's usual screed (as he usually ends most episodes of *Real Time*), he followed this commentary by performing the "world's first unbaptism." *The Hollywood Reporter* summarized the ritual thus:

> Donning a sorcerer's hat and wielding a magic wand, Maher then produced a black and white photograph of Davies, on which he performed his mystical ritual. The brief ceremony was made complete with references to Laverne and Shirley, Harry Potter and The Blair Witch Project. "By the power granted in me by the Blair Witch," he declared, "I call upon the Mormon spirits to leave your body the fuck alone. . . . Brother Edward, in this world you had to put up with Mitt Romney," he concluded. "You've suffered enough."

This "unbaptism" clearly represents one of Webber's "flashpoints." Linda Hutcheon describes the role of parody on a postmodern cultural moment,

"Postmodern parody . . . is always inextricably bound to social discourse" (204). Maher's routine captured the zeitgeist of one element of the 2012 US elections as some left-leaning secularists were suspicious of how Romney's religious background might manifest itself should he become president. Furthermore, Maher specifically was part of the immediate reaction to the news of the Davies posthumous baptism along with similar reports about Holocaust victims and survivors. That this revelation of Mormon baptisms was indeed a cultural flashpoint is evidenced in other coverage it received. Other media outlets such as *The Last Word* with Lawrence O'Donnell, the YouTube channel The Young Turks, and *The Colbert Report* also did stories on the topic around this same time. Jonathan Greenberg describes this function of the late-night news satire genre as functioning, "simultaneously as sources of the news, satiric comments upon it, and parodies of the way that it is covered" (266). In this flashpoint, Maher, Colbert, and others served all three of these functions.

For another example of a comedian reacting to the reports of the practice of the Mormon posthumous baptism, in his comedy special *Relatively Well*, Dave Foley ranted about this as well, bringing up the 100,000 deceased people of Jewish faith who have received baptism by proxy. Foley adds, "They baptized Ann Frank nine times, bitch just would not take." Webber insists, "comedy is about power, whether most comedians at present would like to admit it or not. . . . It can be a way to inspire people to think outside the box: good comedy does that" (*The Cultural Set Up of Comedy* 190).

Returning to parody religions and rituals, Stephen Colbert also responded to the news of the Davies posthumous baptism by staging a parody ritual on February 23, 2012. After doing his usual masterful job of satirizing this Mormon practice, he then converted all dead Mormons to Judaism. To accomplish this, "Since Jews do not baptize, I will now proxy circumcise all the dead Mormons," Colbert declared. He made Jay the intern hold a hot dog, which was then inserted into a cigar cutter. Colbert formally stated, "By the power invested in me by renting *Yentl*, I hereby circumcise every dead Mormon in the name of the Father, and that's it." Chop! While eating the tip he had just cut off the hot dog, he says, "Congratulations dead Mormons, you are now dead Jews. I just hope no one baptizes you without your permission."

Another variation on parody religions comes from Australian comedian and television presenter John Safran. Safran produced and starred in a comedic travel documentary called *John Safran vs God* (2004). It is an eight-part series in which he visits a wide variety of religious people and joins in their practices. He is for the most part earnest and open-minded. While meeting people he does not enact the Maher posture of Doubting Thomas but rather attempts to remain open to these many experiences. For example, the series's final episode is dedicated to one encounter, in which he is the recipient of an exorcism by fundamentalist preacher Bob Larson. The Christian group expresses concern over his participating in so many other pagan activities in the making of the show. This episode has been remarked upon by the lack of commentary from Safran on the sincerity of his participation. But, in the show he certainly appears to be a fully engaged participant. In later interviews he simply said it was very intense and he doesn't really remember many of the details.

During *John Safran vs God*, in addition to his travelogue, he also adds comedic wrap-arounds and comedy skits which are edited around the visits and interviews. One of these skits is called the "Atheist door-knocking skit." The whole bit is meant as a parody of the door-to-door missionary work of Mormons. The segment begins with one of his wrap-arounds. These typically feature him sitting comfortably by a fire with a robe or smoking jacket on, brandy in hand, musing out loud about religion. In this segment, he complains about missionary Mormons and their reputation as early-morning door knockers.

He begins with a disclaimer on tolerance.

> I'm tolerant. I'm the mahat-mafuckin-gandhi of tolerance. I don't care what you believe, how you dress, or who you bang. . . . I don't care if you think Christ is the Messiah. I don't care if you think Christ is the Antichrist, I don't care if you think you're the Messiah. . . . Care factor: 0!

After a little more on this theme of apathetic-tolerance, he then reveals the one thing he does care about:

> Do whatever you want to do, just don't knock on my door before mid-day on Saturday. . . . I'm looking at you, Mormons! . . . Maybe I was out living a little, maybe I was out till 5 in the morning drinking Kahlúa and milk, and dancing to Yaz and the Plastic Population. You didn't think about that, did you? You didn't factor Yaz into your little plan to ring my bell at 8 in the morning. I don't remember that bit in the New Testament where Jesus says onto his flock to go around and annoy the shit out of people by bashing on their door. I must have overlooked Deuteronomy 13:11 "Blessed is the man who goes around banging on people's doors at all hours of the morning, for he truly is Jesus's little friend."

This rant serves as segue into the skit.

The skit itself shows Safran walking around a neighborhood in Salt Lake City knocking on people's doors trying to preach to them about Atheism. He is dressed in black pants and a clean white shirt. His director joins him, so they are a pair in the fashion of Mormon door-to-door missionaries. He has pamphlets that contain the lyrics to the XTC song "Dear God," he has a copy of Darwin's *Origin of the Species*, and they wear badges that have their names as well as the word "Atheist." John shows all this to the camera, saying, "I've got my atheist badge, let's do some good." The next two minutes are a montage of the two of them ringing doorbells and trying to tell people about Atheism.

Some people slam the door in their face. One person yells, "Take us off of your list!" (whatever that means?) One person tells them that he is a Bishop in the LDS church. One elderly man hits John with a rake. Some people do patiently listen, as John tells them things like, "Us Atheists believe the Bible isn't true and it's all just stories" and "We follow the teachings of a man named Charles Darwin." Safran tells one patient woman who is holding a baby in her arms, "Did you know your relatives are monkeys?" He then reads to the young mother XTC lyrics, "Dear God, You're always letting us humans down/ The wars you bring, the babes you drown."

At other doors, he tells people, "Did you know that when you die, your body just decomposes into the earth and nothing happens. There's no soul, there's no Heaven, God is meaningless." He tells people that religion causes anxiety and that Atheism can "cure you of this anxiety." The skit culminates with a montage of Safran yelling at doors that have been slammed in his face things like, "Did we disturb you from your sleep?" and "Sorry, were you enjoying your own private time and it was really intrusive of someone to come bashing on your door and push their beliefs on you?!"

The entire skit is an act out lampooning the idea of going door to door to proselytize. The satire here functions by identifying this activity and then exaggerating it by extending it into a sphere where it *prima facie* ceases to make sense. It is a clear example of acting out the rhetorical strategy of lampooning through the strategy of *reducto ad absurdum*. When the audience see Atheists trying to be door-to-door preachers, one realizes how absurd the entire pursuit is.

On his weekly HBO show *Last Week Tonight*, on August 16, 2015, John Oliver announced his recently formed and very real new Megachurch, Our Lady of the Perpetual Exemption. This parody church was part of that episode's report on some of the questionable practices of some megachurches and some televangelists. Daniel Kreps reported this summary in *Rolling Stone*:

> After highlighting a list of egregious instances of abuse by prosperity preachers, Oliver noted how difficult it was for the IRS to regulate the activities of these churches because the rules concerning religious organizations are so "purposely broad" and "a little vague." In the IRS Tax Guide for Churches 7 Religious Organizations "the term church is found, but not specifically defined" and the "IRS makes no attempt to evaluate the content of whatever doctrine a particular organization claims in religious, provided the particular beliefs are truly and sincerely held and the practices are not illegal."
>
> ("John Oliver shuts down fake church over Unsolicited Semen"
> September 14, 2015)

In addition to highlighting the questionable relationship between these disreputable churches and the IRS, Oliver also explained the practice of seed money and the so-called prosperity gospel.

> Oliver targeted the fraternity of shady televangelists fleecing Americans for millions. . . . These hucksters demand "seed" money from their followers in exchange for the lord's blessing and then use said seed money to treat themselves to lavish private jets, vacations, and luxurious "parsonages" in the form of mega-mansions. Oh, and to make matters worse, all of these donations and purchases are tax-free under the guise of religious exemptions.
> (Marlow Stern "John Oliver's Bogus Church a Huge Success: 'Thousands of Dollars' Received" *The Daily Beast* August 24, 2015)

Thus, following his usual extended segment on the subject, Oliver moved to a nearby set that had the cheesy, homey look one sometimes associates with televangelists. To help set the scene he is met there by the character of Wonder Jo, his televangelist wife played by Rachel Dratch. Her makeup and style suggest a Tammy-Faye-Baker-inspired look. In the guise of these characters, they ask the viewers to send them "seeds." John Oliver claims that he has received a prophecy and that the "Viewers at home must plant a seed." Wonder Jo then joins in, "Preferably in the form of cash though we do take checks."

"Please do not send us actual seeds," Oliver adds. Wonder Jo, ever echoing Oliver, emphasizes laughing, "We ain't interested in your seeds!" Oliver continues, "Please send us your actual money . . . if you do this, and this is real, great things will happen to you, and that is apparently something I am allowed to say." This is followed by the two of them acting out a faith healing. Joined by a gospel choir, Oliver then shouts, "Truly we have witnessed a miracle tonight, give us money!"

That this is a parody meant to lampoon televangelists in general and the practice of prosperity gospel specifically is clear. This routine by Oliver had several unexpected twists. The first was that his show really did incorporate a real church. He did this to illustrate how easy it was to do and that everything in his parody was in fact technically legal. Second, many people did in fact send in money. *Rolling Stone* reported that he raised "thousands of dollars" (Kreps "John Oliver shuts down fake church over Unsolicited Semen" September 14, 2015). Any money raised was later donated to Doctors without Borders. Going further, despite explicitly asking their viewers not to send in actual seeds, they received a lot of the stuff. They also received other odd paraphernalia, such as t-shirts and bobbleheads. And finally, they received another type of seed which they decided was reason enough to formally close their church. The closing is explained in a letter posted to the church's associated website. In this letter, Oliver explains:

We have still, miraculously, not broken any laws by promising you untold riches in return for sending us money. We're also not closing down because you all kept sending us actual seeds, even though we explicitly told you not to. We're closing because multiple people sent us sperm through the mail. And when someone sends you jizz through the mail, it's time to stop whatever you're doing. So we are shutting this s**t down.
(www.ourladyofperpetualexemption.com/)

Laycock suggests that parody religions demand comparisons, and this was clearly a function of Oliver's Our Lady of the Perpetual Exemption. "The most enthusiastic parody religions often have a political agenda. They seek not only to interrogate the category for religion but the implications of this category on public policy" (21). By establishing a real-in-the-legal-sense church, Oliver forced his audience to ask uncomfortable questions about religion. This includes the highly questionable practices of some televangelists as well as the actual legal mechanisms that protect them. One more factor that makes the comedy of Oliver's rhetoric work is his deconstruction of the word seed. From literal seeds, to the televangelist-usage of a spiritual seed, to sperm, the word is hilariously and dialogically deconstructed, helping lampoon the religious practice of prosperity gospel.

Both parody religions and act outs voicing the incarnate are comedic exercises in *redcuto ad absurdum*. The humorist takes some aspects of religion, belief, hypocrisy, and so on and exaggerates it both for humorous effect and to make a point of some sort. The point is McGraw's violation, the laughter keeps an element of the benign, and the resultant ridicule creates space for charged humor and social justice.

Though it would be hard to enumerate, anthropologists have estimated that there are currently 10,000 different religions on the earth today, and maybe 1 million since the dawn of civilization. Are they all just variations on the same theme, what Patton Oswalt characterized as the "old sky cake dodge"? There are simply too many variables to land on a precise number, but do the people counting include parody religions in their count? Are joke religions also religions? Currently on the "About" section of the website for the Church of the Flying Spaghetti Monster is a section of "Questions and Answers," one of which is "Q: Is this a joke?" The answer provided is:

It's not a joke. Elements of our religion are sometimes described as satire and there are many members who do not literally believe our scripture, but this isn't unusual in religion. A lot of Christians don't believe the Bible is literally true – but that doesn't mean they aren't True Christians.

If you say Pastafarians must believe in a literal Flying Spaghetti Monster to be True Believers, then you can make a similar argument for Christians. There is a lot of outlandish stuff in the Bible that rational Christians choose to ignore.

(www.venganza.org/about/ August 10, 2019)

Is it a joke, or not? Neither or both? After all, multivariant figures are also an integral element in joke telling. For the audience, the reception and interpretation of humor is at times complex. At its essence, one never knows with certainty if one particular utterance or another is meant to be taken seriously or not. Jim Jefferies once described a critic who included quotes from his act in print, and even Jeffries admitted that taken out of a performance context, the meaning is lost. "See, if you read my material . . . it's a bad read" (*Freedumb*). If an individual comment or joke without the usual contextual clues of the playful nature is cherry-picked then the comedian's art in danger of being lost. There is no certainty, which is rather the point. A comedic utterance is both serious and silly. In this sense it is akin to the famous duck-rabbit, or other such multivariant images. These optical illusions are created in such a way as they can be interpreted as one or an alternate image. In the case of the duck-rabbit, the viewer can see the drawing either of a duck or of a rabbit, and as the brain attempts to decipher which the image is, it, in effect, flips back and forth between the two. Similarly, a joke is also a multivariant experience. Often there are contextual clues, such as being in a comedy club, or the laughter of others, or being told, "this is a joke." Even the common structure of a joke (set-up/punch line) provides a contextual clue. It is ultimately up to each individual in the moment to recognize that it is a joke. (This is to say nothing as to whether or not one finds a particular joke funny, or well written, or well told.)

Parody religions function as the duck-rabbit. In *Performance Theory*, Richard Schechner described the actor in character as "not Hamlet but not not Hamlet" (190). A parody religion is not a religion but also not not a religion. It is existentially multivariant. This very tension partly creates the humor. This ambiguity partially creates the pointed social commentary.

5 Comedians Satirizing Creationists

"I Needed to Go to This Tabernacle of Ignorance"

On his 2011 comedy album *This Has to Be Funny*, Marc Maron includes a routine in which he describes a visit to the Creation Museum, located in Petersburg, Kentucky, just south of Cincinnati (http://creationmuseum.org/). Not his first critique of it, on November 14, 2010, Maron broadcast an episode of his *WTF* podcast largely recorded inside the Creation Museum during a visit. Both include Maron's typical combination of smart and angry, as he satirizes the Museum and its agenda. Thus, Marc Maron provides an insightful and witty critique of the absurd world of the Creation Museum, a monologue illustrative of the power and the nature of religious satire. This criticism takes the form of describing some of the Museum's displays and then reacting to them (the standard "joke formula" explained in Chapter 2). The displays he spends the most time critiquing include the Garden of Eden room, animatronics of Old Testament figures, and the Noah's Ark room. Other comedians have also treated the subject of the Creation Museum; Bill Maher in particular has a segment in his film *Religulous*(2008) where he visits the Museum and interviews its president Ken Ham.

On *This Has to Be Funny*, Maron lambasts the ignorance of the Museum, as he sets the scene for his visit:

> I needed to go, I needed to go for the wrong reasons, obviously, but I needed to witness. I needed to go to this tabernacle of ignorance. And I went there thinking, I am going to go there, I am going to be horrified, you know, gonna be angry, smug, condescending, righteous, you know pompous even, and just judging these fucking idiots that are going there for what they see as the right reason.

This is in essence the routine's basic premise – Maron's persona of angry social commentator, visiting this "tabernacle of ignorance" in order to see just how offended he can get. Later in the routine, he also summarizes the creationist agenda as he sees it: as he puts it, they believe

> that the world is about 6,000 years old. Now human beings as we know them, are roughly . . . they probably really kinda come about 250

thousand years ago. Dinosaurs that they're talking about, probably about what 300 million years ago. So the gap they're trying to close is a good 300 million year gap, that they're just trying to close up with pseudoscience and interesting dioramas.

(*This Has to Be Funny*)

The ignorance, as I labeled it, of the museum is its patently erroneous depiction of the history of life on Earth cojoined with its scientifically baseless attack on evolution. One might find it odd that a comedian would defend science, but in the culture of post-September 11 satire, this in fact became a common topic for some comedians. This is another clear way that the satiric agenda paralleled a major concern of the New Atheists. Defending science in general and evolution in particular clearly motivated some New Atheists writers. For example, here Sam Harris succinctly explains the fact of evolution:

All complex life one Earth has developed from simpler life-forms over billions of years. This is a fact that no longer admits of intelligent dispute. If you doubt that human beings evolved from prior species, you may as well doubt that the sun is a star.

(*Letter to a Christian Nation* 68)

The Creation Museum is a missionary project of the religious organization Answers in Genesis (AiG), run by well-known creationist Ken Ham. AiG is an anti-evolution group, and of course, the Museum represents their propaganda. The Museum opened in May 2007 and, as of May 2023, their website claims that they have had 3.5 million visitors. A visit to their website shows the Museum's attempt to be perceived as a museum of science. That the Creation Museum values Biblical interpretation over scientific fact is made clear in statements similar to the one that opens the homepage of their website:

The state-of-the-art 70,000 square foot museum brings the pages of the Bible to life, casting its characters and animals in dynamic form and placing them in familiar settings. Adam and Eve live in the Garden of Eden. Children play and dinosaurs roam near Eden's Rivers.

(http://creationmuseum.org/ accessed January 1, 2014)

AiG's role in the Museum is not clearly advertised to the casual visitor. On their website and in the main galleries of the Museum, there is no direct reference to Answers in Genesis, nor to the Museum being a "ministry," which is what it is legally classified as. The on-site book shop does have some literature from AiG. And, their human resources job application page includes this requirement of all job seekers:

> In order to preserve the function and integrity of the Answers in Genesis (AiG) ministry (and its various attractions and outreaches, both domestic and international) in its mission to proclaim the absolute truth and authority of Scripture and to provide a biblical role model to our employees and to the global body of Christ, the community, and society at large, it is imperative that all persons employed by the AiG ministry in any capacity, or who serve as volunteers, should abide by and agree to our Statement of Faith and conduct themselves accordingly.
> (May 2023, "The AiG Statement of Faith," www.answersingenesis.org/about/faith)

This statement includes the assertion:

> The 66 books of the Bible are the written Word of God. The Bible is divinely inspired and inerrant throughout. Its assertions are factually true in all the original autographs. It is the supreme authority in everything it teaches. Its authority is not limited to spiritual, religious, or redemptive themes but includes its assertions in such fields as history and science.

And, on Ken Ham's website, he explains his basic view on dinosaurs, "There is no mystery surrounding dinosaurs if you accept the Bible's totally different account of dinosaur history."

> According to the Bible: Dinosaurs first existed around 6,000 years ago. God made the dinosaurs, along with the other land animals, on Day 6 of the Creation Week (Genesis 1:20–25, 31). Adam and Eve were also made on Day 6 – so dinosaurs lived at the same time as people, not separated by eons of time. Dinosaurs could not have died out before people appeared because dinosaurs had not previously existed; and death, bloodshed, disease, and suffering are a result of Adam's sin (Genesis 1:29–30; Romans 5:12, 14; 1 Corinthians 15:21–22).
> ("Are dinosaurs a mystery?" <https://answersingenesis.org/dinosaurs/when-did-dinosaurs-live/what-really-happened-to-the-dinosaurs/> accessed May 12, 2019, italics in original)

When Maron begins his routine, he immediately takes his audience on a surprise turn, for when he describes his arrival at the Museum, he admits to being impressed. His first reaction is, "I walked in and thought this is pretty cool; a lot of money went into making this, they're really selling this." Rhetorically, stand-up comedians sometimes preface religious satire with some kind of parameters that serve to build rapport with the audience in which they seem – if not objective – perhaps less angry or judgmental. As an additional example, when John Oliver announced the creation of his Megachurch Our Lady of the Perpetual Exemption as part of lampooning televangelists who ask for seed money, he began his report with a sort of disclaimer, stating:

> There are roughly 350,000 congregations in the United States, and many of them do great work: feeding the hungry, clothing the poor. But this story is not about them. This is about the churches that exploit people's faith for monetary gain.

This rhetorical device allows the comedian to satirize whatever religious subject is their theme while reassuring the audience in front of them that the comedian is not judging them directly. Rather, others are being judged, the extremists and the hypocrites. In this case, it allows Maron to freely satirize the Museum without the audience judging him for being so judgmental. Furthermore, in this particular example, beginning with this kind of empathy may also represent a more mature version of the Marc Maron stage persona.

Naturally, not all comedians make this rhetorical gesture. Though it is meant to create a safe space for the audience to participate in the communal act of laughter, some comedians intentionally do the opposite. They aggressively include the audience among those being judged. Doug Stanhope does this and so does Jim Jefferies. In his comedy special *Contraband* (2008), during an atheistic rant, Jefferies directly calls out the audience, declaring, "If you're religious, you're a fuckin' idiot, alright? Point blank, the guy in the cloud, and all that, you're a fuckin' moron. Read a science book, watch a Richard Dawkins documentary, you dumb fuckin' cunt, right."

For most comics, every description leads to a reaction. As told to me in private communications, comedy teacher Chili Challis explains that it is in the reaction that the performer's persona is experienced. In other words, any comedian might describe the Creation Museum, but only Marc Maron will react to it the way Marc Maron would. And, according to Challis, this reaction is also what is commonly called the punch line. So, it is in Maron's (unique) reactions that most of the humor is to be found.

Maron's reaction to this pseudoscientific menagerie is at times outrage but more often a willingness to experience the journey of the Museum on its own terms – that is, to learn what he can about the people who take it seriously, or as Maron puts it, "these fucking idiots that are going there for what they see is the right reason." For example, his reaction to seeing a dinosaur eating a pineapple is not umbrage, but mock curiosity: "because I was so hooked into the narrative of the Museum I was like. . . . I hope they can explain why that carnivorous ancient reptile would be enjoying some vegetables."

In his essay "On Laughter," Henri Bergson describes "*mechanical inelasticity*" (italics in original, 5), suggesting that one of the sources of the comedic is the living made mechanical. Laughter is caused by something "mechanical encrusted on the living" (18). Any form of behavior or logic that is so formalized as to make our human potential rigid clashes "with the inner suppleness of life" (22). He claims, "It is rigidity that society eyes with suspicion" (68). This rigidity – the mechanical – the idealizing of myth over life – these exact circumstances embody the pseudoscientific literalness proffered by the Creation Museum. It is quite literally the religious ideas of young earth creationists made mechanical: made mechanical in the dioramas and animatronics Maron et al. so adeptly critique. Certainly, believers invested in the ideas of one or another dogma may participate in perpetuating the myth of a monologic meaning, but the meaning itself is never solely in the utterance.

Thus, the illusion of monologic authority of dogmatic religious utterances will always be subject to satire, as comic writers and comedians create their own meaning through dialogic gamesmanship and willful misreading. This is in complete accord with Northrop Frye's explanation of satire as "inconvenient truth: Philosophies of life abstract from life, and an abstraction implies the leaving out of inconvenient data. The satirist brings up these inconvenient data" (229). The Creation Museum's dioramas and displays demonstrates their own avoidance of inconvenient data in living machines, and Marc Maron and others find the humor in satirizing the abundant absurdities that result. Frye goes on to demonstrate that attacks on both pseudoscience and religion have a long history in satire and comic writing.

Museums often employ what Barbara Kirsehblatt-Gimblett has described as either *in situ* or *in context* display strategies, but both of these rhetorical devices seem to fail in the pseudoscientific position advocated by the Museum. *In situ* museum displays exhibit artifacts and ideas in artistically realistic replicas of cultural situations, rooms, locales, etc. Recreations of historic rooms with authentic objects combined with replicas would be an example. *In context*, displays coordinate their exhibits around controlling theoretical ideas, such as historic or aesthetic themes. These terms "call into question the nature of the whole, the burden of interpretation, and the location of meaning" (Kirsehblatt-Gimblett 19). By attempting to create such realistically rendered dioramas, models, and animatronics, the Creation Museum seems to be practicing some form of *in situ* mimetic display strategy. However, the overall lack of authentic objects to display in fact renders it more of an *in context* rhetoric. That is, the museum prioritizes its own theoretical (i.e., dogmatic) position over the inconvenient truth of accurate scientific data. They try to teach visitors how to interpret various scientific premises within a creationist framework, creating a fantasy environment reminiscent of Jean Baudrillard's hyperreality.

The dogma of the religious creationist epitomizes Bergsonian inelasticity. Regardless of their potential impact on the social sphere, this ardent monologism make a very clear manifestation of this comedic tension: their dogma remains inflexible in the face of other data (scientific, philosophical, legal, or even theological). The Creation Museum, therefore, takes this monologic comedic quality and makes itself even more apparent by the creation of their three-dimensional displays. When one sees a triceratops with a saddle, when one sees a brontosaurus on Noah's ark, when ones see a tyrannosaurus eating a pineapple, when one sees a penguin in the Garden of Eden, the monologic inflexibility is immediately mockable. It is not just that the idea is laughable – it is more – it is that the inflexibility of the rhetorical argument is laughable.

The Creation Museum's literally mechanical representation of their dogmatic beliefs is what Mikhail Bakhtin meant by monologic. Authoritative utterances attempt to fix meaning. Meaning is not fixed, but rather co-created between text and reader, speaker and listener. "The word in living conversation is directly, blatantly, oriented toward a future answer-word" (Morris, *The Bakhtin Reader* 76). Thus, Bakhtinian dialogics situates meaning as co-created in the moment of social context. Certainly, believers invested in the ideas of one or another dogma may participate in perpetuating the myth of a monologic meaning, but the meaning itself is never solely in the utterance. As Michael Holquist summarizes it, "Dialogue is real, monologue is not; at worse, monologue is an illusion, as when it is uncritically taken for granted" (59).

This thorough self-proclaimed literal interpretation of the Bible resulting in a fantasy environment ably brings to mind Baudrillard's model of the simulacra, a fourth order simulation: "it has no relation to any reality whatsoever, it is its own pure simulacrum" (6). It embodies the hyperreal, "the generation of the real without origin or reality" (1), and this is exactly what visitors find in the Creation Museum's agenda as revealed by their animatronics. By recreating not only a religious mythology but also a re-interpreted religious dogma, the Museum no longer even refers to its own traditional scripture. This entire museum exemplifies the postmodern hyperreal due to the irony of the creationist claim to biblical authority – even though the Bible makes no mention of dinosaurs! There are no dinosaurs in Genesis – thus why does AiG insist on building an entire museum to suggest that there were? Baudrillard describes religion in general as, "an uninterrupted circuit without reference or circumference" (6). If religion exists within such an "uninterrupted circuit" then satirists such as Maron do indeed interrupt this circuit! Comedians attempt to short circuit religion's self-referential and circular logic, highlighting and ridiculing absurdities.

The Bill Maher film *Religulous* includes a segment where Maher visits the Creation Museum shortly before the Museum opens. A shot of the triceratops with a saddle is one of the most popular segments in the film. When Maher sees it, he quips, "Wow-that's a saddle." In addition to the tour Maher receives, Ken Ham himself appears describing the mission and goals of the

Museum. Maher asks Ham to explain the importance of the Museum's premise that dinosaurs and humans coexisted: "If you're saying this part over here [in the Bible], it says God made land animals and man on the same day is not true, then ultimately, why should I believe this bit over here?"

In the interview, Ham explains, "This is a God, he's an infinite God, he's not always working in ways we understand." Maher, ever the doubter, then challenges him, "Don't you think that's a cop-out?" Ham answers, "He is God. Are you God?" After an awkward pause, Maher answers simply, "No." Note the stark contrast between Maher's line of questioning and Ham's answer. Maher has prefigured these types of encounters in his film. When confronted with certainty, he offers doubt. Ham eschews doubt, explaining his faith in an "infinite god." Here, the viewer confronts a classical situation of doubt as explained by Glenn Most above: two clearly incompatible views that one must choose between. By his performance of doubt, Maher succeeds in creating both humorous satire and firebomb after firebomb. Ham is clearly made uncomfortable by Maher's questions of doubt and seems unable to answer.

The evolution debate was front and center during the 2007 Republican primaries. In the first Republican debate, held on May 3, 2007, in Simi Valley, California, candidates were asked point blank if they did not believe in evolution. John Oliver was present and described what happened during his 2008 special *Terrifying Times*.

> I did get to witness one incredible moment of political theatre when all 10 at that point potential leaders of the free world were asked the same question, and that question was, "Who here doesn't believe in evolution?" And three of those men raised their hands. And then, none of those three men put their hands down and said "Only joking."

The three candidates who self-identified as evolution deniers were Governor Mike Huckabee, Senator Sam Brownback, and Representative Tom Tancredo.

Oliver explained the issue a little more: there are "groups that want us to put stickers on the front of all school science textbooks explaining that evolution is only one possible theory of life on earth." To illustrate the ridiculousness of the suggestion, he suggests a sticker for the Bible, "Of course, this could all be bullshit. Maybe he never died. Perhaps he opened a donkey sanctuary. He had a clear bond with donkeys." In his 2006 article for CNN, Simon Hooper noted recent attempts by Creationists to force their agenda into public schools is an example of religious ideas that have "increasingly impinged on public life in ways unacceptable to New Atheist rationalism" (www.cnn.com/2006/WORLD/europe/11/08/atheism.feature/index.html).

This biblical literalism embodies the mechanical encrusted over the living. The inability or unwillingness of creationists like Ham to evolve their interpretations of scripture with developments in culture and science shows a mechanical style of thinking, one that is unwilling to engage in true debate. They may doll up their ideology in contemporary rhetorical styles, such as this very Museum itself, but it is the very depiction of their ideology in the vernacular of the Museum that betrays their actual crustiness. It demonstrates the very "pseudo"-ness of their science. It is the Bergsonian crust, it invites laughter and ridicule due to being so inhumanly mechanistic. It is a Chucky Cheese Band version of theology recalling Colbert's parody of this kind of limited thinking described in Chapter 2.

This creationist notion of people and dinosaurs living together has provided fodder for numerous comedians besides Maron and Maher. For example, Bill Hicks, Lewis Black, Robin Ince, and Eddie Izzard have all done routines based on the comic potential of this anachronistic suggestion. In his 1993 comedy special *Revelations*, Bill Hicks said, "If the world is 12000 years old, and dinosaurs existed, and they existed in that time, you would think it would have been mentioned in the fucking Bible." He tells a story of what it would have been like for Jesus and the disciples to meet a brontosaurus. Hicks also brings up another common issue raised by creationists, the quandary of the dinosaur fossil. In separate routines, both Hicks and Black satirize the creationist suggestion that fossils exist as a test to faith. In his 2006 HBO special *Red, White, and Screwed*, Black in particular takes time to outline some of his thinking as a Jewish person, promising that any Jew will gladly take time out of their day to explain the Old Testament to any Christian who wants to understand it properly. Black's rant includes the comment, "These people are watching *The Flintstones* as if it were a documentary."

This mechanization of Creationist beliefs opens another humorous strategy Maron deploys which is to reinterpret some of the exhibits in a way that lays bare the biases of the Museum's creators. For example, on *This Has to Be Funny* Maron describes what he considers the anti-Semitic feeling of depicting Old Testament figures as obvious Jewish stereotypes. Maron first observes this tendency when he is describing the gallery "Biblical Authority." He describes it as "a display room you know about the old testament and the new testament, and they had these audio-animatronics," and he immediately notes something about these lifelike dolls:

> [O]n the left side of the room you had Isaiah, you had Moses with his commandments, you had Abraham who was pensive and sitting for some reason and had a harp-like instrument, I don't know why. And they couldn't have looked more Jew-y.

To Maron, these Old Testament animatronics depict stereotypical Jewish physical traits, and he is offended by the anti-Semitic implications of this. Rhetorically, his ire is his punch line. "I was like, you've got to be kidding me! I mean it might as well have been Sid Caesar, Gabe Kaplan and Richard Lewis sitting there. And the plaque should have read 'JEWS FROM THE PAST!'" He goes on to suggest they might as well as be eating bagels and playing music from *Fiddler on the Roof*.

In his related *WTF* podcast, Maron along with Ryan Singer and Geoff Tate record from within the Creation Museum, commenting on what they saw as they saw it. The broadcast included a reflections-style segment near the end during which they gave their overall impressions. They remarked upon the quality of the Museum's displays, especially the detail in the Noah's Ark gallery impressed them, calling it "phenomenal." On *This Has to Be Funny*, Maron describes one model's depiction of the parade of animals:

> They're on the ramp, on the ramp going up to the ark, there's little animals; look at this, oh! Two giraffes, two zebras, two lions, two brontosauruses; but you're mind doesn't stop there you're just onto the pigs. Brontosauruses on the ark! I'm good with that!

They found such displays thought-provoking, describing the Museum as a form of sophisticated confusion that did a "very good job of propagandizing their point" and might well succeed on somebody on the fence. Maron declares at one point, "Oh it's all explained, my mind is significantly fucked!" (*This Has to Be Funny*).

How is an audience meant to receive Maron's satire? His core fans already know him to be atheistic with other religious satire on previous comedy albums, so they perhaps already heed his message. Of course, stand-up itself is primarily a monologist's art form and therefore certainly has its own monologic-dialogic tensions. At any rate, Maron uses his on-stage persona as angry and intelligent as a platform to provide insightful observations and to perform outraged reactions (a la Chili Challis's model of character-based premises and punch lines). The literalness of the Museum's own displays embody the Bergsonian aesthetic of the living being encrusted with the mechanical being one source of laughter. As Bakhtin suggests, "However monologic the utterance may be . . . it cannot but be, in some measure, a response to what has already been said about the given subject . . . the utterance is filled with dialogic overtones" (Morris, *The Bakhtin Reader* 86). Thus, authority may attempt monologic utterances, but meaning is ultimately dialogic. Satirists like Maron can exploit this dissonance between the Museum's attempts to portray biblical authority with anger, irony, and humor. Religious utterances are among the most monologic, making the whole genre prime for satire. And as Maron critiques the Museum on *This Has to be Funny*, he also relishes the spirit behind the Museum, declaring with loving irony:

> But I left, not angry at them, not angry at the Museum, not angry at the people that were there. I was sort of elated, I felt sort of gloriously

embarrassed for our country. But I felt deeply proud to be an American because I realized that what I was standing in the parking lot of could only happen in America. These are our fucking morons; and they've done a beautiful thing down there.

[A] magic man done it!

– Robin Ince

In a 2007 segment for the British sketch comedy show *Comedy Cuts*, Robin Ince does a routine that uses the comic approach of *reducto ad asdsurbdum* of lampooning a questionable idea by exaggerating it to satirically demonstrate the irrationality of the Creationist position. A video clip of the segment is now available on YouTube under the title "Robin Ince on Creationism" (2007/03/15 on ITV in the UK <www.youtube.com/watch?v=KdocQHsPCNM> accessed January 6, 2020).

The clip features Ince presenting a comic monologue, with two additional performers: one playing the accordion to add comical music cues to his narrative, the other a sort of mime who acts out some of the elements he mentions during the monologue. Ince introduces his subject with the claim, "The History of Creationist Thought." Lasting approximately three minutes, during the monologue he describes the debate as an encounter between one character who represents science and another representing creationism. They ask each other to summarize their positions. Science goes first and explains how the scientific method supports the findings of evolution. He presents the age of the earth, amino acids, early life-forms adapting to their environment, and eventually says, "and thus we end up here." After an awkward pause, the Creationism character says simply, "Our theory is this: magic man done it!" The Scientist responds, "'Magic man done it' isn't science." Disappointed, the Creationists gives a despondent "oh."

Twenty years go by in Ince's story and then the Creationist returns.

Sorry about last time, we hadn't really thought it out, but now we have come back with a proper scientific theory . . . the theory of Intelligent Design. Not stupid design, not idiot design, not banana design . . . in fact, if you don't get it, Mr. Scientist, maybe it's 'cause you're not intelligent enough!

The scientist asks for the new theory. In reply, the Creationist repeats back nearly word-for-word Ince's earlier explanation of evolution. In this portion, it is worth noting that the musician and the mime basically repeat all the same accents, which goes to underscore how much the creationist is simply repeating the earlier description of evolution. After repeating, "and thus we end up here," the Scientist calls out the creationist for stealing their theory. The Creationist begrudgingly admits that there is one difference but is reluctant to tell the scientist. The scientist insists, and so finally the Creationist adds, if things in nature sometimes look designed or hard to make, then in those cases, "a magic man done it!"

This concise phrase "a magic man done it" puts its finger directly on why neither creationism nor so-called Intelligent Design function as scientific theories, or even scientific ideas at all. "Creation-science is scientific in name only. It is a thinly disguised religious position rather than a theory to be tested using scientific methods" (Shermer 141). In his routine, Ince makes much use of the word theory, and this aspect of his routine identifies another integral part of the public debate on evolution: misuse of the word "theory." Creationists in the early 2000s often attempt to deride evolution by using the phrase "it's just a theory" to create confusion about its certainty. For example, former conservative Presidential hopefuls Rick Perry and Michelle Bachman have misused the word "theory" in an attempt to attack evolution and elevate Intelligent Design (Perry did so at a campaign event in New Hampshire in 2011 and Bachman did so while speaking at the University of Iowa in 2011. Perry: <https://talkingpointsmemo.com/dc/perry-on-evolution-it-s-a-theory-that-s-out-there-video?ref=fpa>; Bachman: <www.youtube.com/watch?v=JuENKYHuUY8&feature=emb_logo>).

This concern about the misuse of the word theory has been sounded by Dawkins, Hitchens, and Harris. For example, in *God Is Not Great*, Christopher Hitchens described religious intelligent designers as misusing the word, writing that they

> unwisely say that evolutionary biology is "only a theory," which betrays their ignorance of the meaning of the word "theory" as well as the meaning of the word "design." A "theory" is something evolved – if you'll forgive the expression – to fit the known facts. It is a successful theory if it survives the introduction of hitherto unknown facts. And it becomes an successful theory if it can make accurate predictions about things or events that have not yet been discovered, or have not yet occurred.
> (85)

Science, Satire, and the New Atheism

Many of the comedians surveyed in this book show their overlapping interests with New Atheism in their preoccupation with defending or explaining science. In *Stripped* (2009), Eddie Izzard described scientists as having "anoraks, they got glasses, they got Bunsen burners, and petri dishes, I gotta go with them." In *Freedumb* (2016), Jim Jefferies compares society to a train moving on a track, and in the engine room dragging us along "are scientists. These are the people that are inventing medicines . . . and finding alternative fuel sources and engineers that are making machines that run more efficiently."

The last car is "50 times bigger," it's full of people dancing around and singing "man on a cloud/ man on a cloud," and "there is so many of these cunts that the train is hardly fucking moving!"

One role the comedians like the ones reviewed in this study and others like them can serve is by creating a very different association. Though potentially divisive, comedians also sometimes have very loyal fan bases. They are found on talk shows, panel shows, and on most streaming platforms, as well as on stage. Though I have described them elsewhere in this study as the vanguard, fighting nightly on the front lines of a rhetorical battle, they are also comparable to greeters who make you feel welcome. With a smile on their faces and a twinkle in their eye, they can make atheism and secular reason seem friendly. If stand-up comedy is essentially a form of conversational storytelling, they can make you laugh while crafting a narrative that is approachable and persuasive. Indeed, the Atheist Atrocities Fallacy came up in the Richard Dawkins documentary *Sex, Death and the Meaning of Life* (2012) while he was interviewing Ricky Gervais. Not only does Gervais bring his sharp comedic insights to the conversation, in a way his charm also uplifts both Dawkins's image and casts Gervais as a poster board for atheism.

Two case studies for the intersection between comedy and science communication are Brian Malow (aka the Science Comedian) and Leighann Lord. Though both have worked for many years as professional stand-up comedians, they both have also found a second career as science communicators. As a comedian, Malow has performed at many science conferences, such as for the American Chemical Society and the National Association of Science Writers. He worked for many years in science communications at the North Carolina Museum of Natural Sciences. And since 2019 has also attended the Lindau Nobel Laureates Meeting and interviewed various scientists. Malow has also contributed to and hosted numerous science outlets, including blogging for *Scientific American*, writing for the podcast *Star Talk* with Neil De Grasse Tyson, and in 2020 produced and hosted a series of YouTube videos about the coronavirus for Sigma Xi, the Scientific Research Honor Society. Malow compared the work of science with the craft of comedy this way, saying of science, "sometimes it is about seeing a pattern no one else saw, comedy is very much like that" (*The Comical Heathen Podcast* S1E15). He added, "There's a growing awareness that science needs to be communicated better, and that's scientists need to communicate what they do better" (*The Comical Heathen Podcast* S1E15).

Leighann Lord is a comedian who in 2019 received the American Humanist Association's Humanists Arts Award. She regularly performs and acts as host to their activities, including hosting their YouTube series. On her website she describes herself as "I'm not religious. I'd like to describe myself as a Humanist but human beings are a hard species to love" (www.veryfunnylady.com/about-me.html). Coincidental with Malow, Lord has also worked with

Neil De Grasse Tyson on *Star Talk*, appearing as a guest co-host. Also, Lord was the face of the African Americans for Humanism Outreach Campaign sponsored by the Center For Inquiry. In 2020 she hosted a series of YouTube lectures produced by the Center for Skeptical Enquiry called Skeptical Inquirer Presents. The outline of some of the ways both Malow and Lord have intersected their comedy careers with science communication serves to illustrate this point of comedy creating an avenue for sharing a diversified and possibly entertaining ingress into the fields of science and reason.

This intersection between New Atheism and comedy as represented by Dawkins and Gervais sharing the screen in *Sex, Death and the Meaning of Life* is essential to understanding the two Reason Rallies. One of the stated goals of the two Reason rallies (2012 and 2016) was to create visibility for the nonreligious. In the same year as the second Rally, Pew reported a doubling of the number of self-reported atheists (up to 7%) as well as nearly one-third of respondents to their surveys claiming no religious affiliations. Yet the demographic remains largely unrepresented in both politics and mainstream popular culture. As reported By Cathy Lynn Grossman in *USA Today*:

> The second worst thing is to go unnoticed and afraid, says *American Atheists* president and rally organizer David Silverman. He estimates that "99% of all atheists are closeted. We have to take back the word 'atheist,' because it has been demonized by critics."
> ("Atheists to cheer for godless USA at 'Reason Rally'" 3/19/2012 <http://usatoday30.usatoday.com/news/religion/story/2012-03-14/atheist-rally-washington-dc/53656042/1>)

Grossman wrote of the gathering, "they plan to head for Washington just like religious groups do – to strut their strength as a voting block, lobby for public policy and raise their social profile." Host and MC Paul Provenza explained another aspect of the event. Interviewed on *Redacted Tonight*, he simply said "It's really just a celebration. It's a party" (www.youtube.com/watch?v=TB9cuubMwA4).

The two Rallies for Reason (2012 and 2016) serve as a kind of nexus for all of these ideas. The 2012 Rally was organized by then-President of the American Atheists David Silverman, they involved speakers from both the world of entertainment and the world of post-September 11 activists for secularism. For example, both Dawkins and Maher were speakers! The list of comedians involved in the two events include several of those already mentioned, such as Provenza and Ian Harris, as well as others like Julia Sweeney and Penn and Teller. Their participation alongside other advocates for science and rationalism, such as Bill Nye and Micheal Shermer, created a public partnership between the two spheres.

6 Conclusion
"People Snapped"

"People snapped."
— Lewis Black

Returning to where this study began, clearly Lewis Black's April 22, 2002 performance of *Comedy Central Presents* exemplifies the layers of satire unearthed throughout. The three spheres of my Venn diagram are present. He provides a satiric takedown of religious dogma as a response to the historic tragic events of September 11. In the introduction, I mentioned how the two seasons of *Comedy Central Presents* following September 11, 2001 had a demonstrable increase in both religious humor as well as comedians who are willing to engage vociferously in charged comedy. In an interview with Lewis Black for my podcast *The Comical Heathen*, I had the opportunity to ask him directly if his episode was some kind of premeditated statement by the producers, to which he replied "No, they're not that smart" (*The Comical Heathen Podcast* S2E8). Instead, to them, it was basically just another episode. If Black's observation is correct, then on its own, this is even more significant. It means that the increases in religious satire during the run of season 6 of *Comedy Central Presents* succinctly represents the very zeitgeist this book has attempted to identify. Rather than being a thought-out plan, it is very likely that, like Black, some comedians were forced to confront the various implications of the tragedy. For example, Dwayne Kennedy quipped:

> After 9–11 . . . Anybody become more spiritual? . . . I started reading the Bible, the Torah, the Quran, back issues of *The Green Lantern*. . . . I was like an atheist with a B plan.
> (*Comedy Central Presents* S7E17 2003)

Religion needed to be commented on in the post-September 11 zeitgeist. It was the same cultural stew that also produced another set of commentators: the so-called New Atheists.

DOI: 10.4324/9781003412854-6

Conclusion

This book has attempted to chart the topic of comedians, comic writers, and other relevant artists whose work in the middle 2000s intersected clearly with the ideas and the agenda of the New Atheists. As reviewed earlier, one must keep in mind that none of the writers usually identified under that umbrella (Dawkins, Hithcens, Harris, etc.) ever called themselves "New Atheists." Instead, as documented above, this was a name given them by journalists and the media, probably beginning with Gary Wolf in his 2006 article "The Church of the Non-Believers." This same basic tenet applies to the comedians included in this study. You will more or less never find any of them self-identifying as "New Atheists." Thus, this book has never attempted to identify any comedians as New Atheist but rather to critique the use of religious satire after September 11 in the context of the zeitgeist Hitchen's mentioned (as quoted earlier). I have analyzed their work in the light of relevant overlapping themes.

In order to detail their work, I have also prioritized a second topic, which is the identification of certain rhetorical strategies common among satirists. These have included an updated definition of satire itself, especially within the broader context of postmodern analysis emphasizing the dialogic nature of language as developed by Mikhail Bakhtin (and his followers). To create both sets of analysis has relied on a great number of examples in an effort to explain and establish the tropes that I have identified as well as placing them within the cultural moment occupied by the "New Atheism."

As this book focuses primarily on the mid-2000s (with some reference to older, historical antecedents), of course, the so-called culture wars have moved on. Even the phrase "New Atheism" is rarely seen in the press anymore, and although there are still comedians in the mold found in this book, it almost seems like the historic moment for religious satire to have its biggest bites has passed. Perhaps, the increased polarization in American politics as engendered by the social media age has resulted in camps wherein hearty religious folks are immune to critique and wherein atheists, agnostics, and skeptics are simply preaching to their own choir. Meanwhile, both sides can play victim, if they want. The looming notion of cancel culture silences some and emboldens others. Since the late 1970s, the Moral Majority movement has made religion increasingly a part of political debate in the United States. Meanwhile, in 2021, the new Secretary of State Antony Blinken took his oath of office on the constitution in lieu of a Bible. Perhaps, he was emboldened by Pastafarian Christopher Schaeffer of the FSM?

The detritus of pop culture gets endlessly recycled by the comedian, the humorist, and the comic writer, as public figures, politicians, religious leaders (religious nuts), and every other talking head that appears in the public sphere insists that they have *the* dogma that *is* the dogma, they get the same treatment Jerry Seinfeld gives to the peanuts provided on airplanes or Henny Youngman gives to his wife – Disrespect. Wordplay uncovers inconsistencies and creates ironies, all in pursuit of the ever-elusive laugh (the bucks follow the laughs, sometimes, but the comic impulse is to mine for laughs).

The comic impulse grapples with religion just as any other topic in the public sphere. No one cares that much about the lone smoker in the privacy of their own home – similarly, the private and personal aspects of religion are rarely in the spotlight of religious satire. Instead, it is the public utterances of leaders, priests, evangelicals, extremists, and other leading citizens who actively seek to impose their religion on the public sphere that draws the comedian's notice. Any target walking through the Parthenon might receive fire, especially in the combat between ideas – bad ideas are like a call to action to some thinkers, and that includes comedians too.

Satire as palimpsest – the writer rubs over what is known with or without what changes the story and challenges the history that is unfolding. In pop culture studies, palimpsest usually refer to "rubbing over," that is like reused monastic scrolls now which the previous writing is still vaguely visible underneath newer scribbles – any pop culture form which recycles or combines the previous with the current might receive this type of labeling or analysis. The comedian's taking of the words or actions of political and religious leaders and ironically deconstructing their monologic utterances is a type of live-action palimpsest. Frye considered it a corrective, one I think that highlights the absurdity of such utterances and actions and then singles out the individuals or groups responsible for public ridicule. It is a corrective in the form of rubbing out parts of what was said or done and overwriting alternative and ironic interpretations which highlight the absurdity. Bad ideas are shown to be bad.

It is a common rejoinder of religious apologists to point to Hitler or Stalin as the consequences of an atheistic worldview. This idea is easily debunked through logic. As Richard Dawkins tweeted on March 2, 2014, "Stalin, Hitler and Saddam Hussein were evil, murdering dictators. All had moustaches. Therefore moustaches are evil." Correlating atheism with murderous dictators is an example of the logical fallacy correlation without causation. In 2014, Michael Shermer wrote an essay dubbing this groundless critique with its own name, The Atheist Atrocities Fallacy (explained here: <https://michaelsherlockauthor.wordpress.com/2014/10/21/the-atheist-atrocities-fallacy-hitler-stalin-pol-pot-in-memory-of-christopher-hitchens/> accessed January 5, 2020). Nonetheless, though a mere paper tiger, it is an oft-repeated worry. For example, in 2006, Dinesh D'Souza wrote:

> In the name of creating their version of a religion-free utopia, Adolf Hitler, Joseph Stalin, and Mao Zedong produced the kind of mass slaughter that no Inquisitor could possibly match. Collectively these atheist tyrants murdered more than 100 million people.
>
> (www.csmonitor.com/2006/1121/p09s01-coop.html accessed January 5, 2020)

The logical reply is that this is specious reasoning. That is, there is no direct relation between these brutal dictators and the possibility that some might have been atheistic. Sam Harris explains:

> People of faith often claim that the crimes of Hitler, Stalin, Mao and Pol Pot were the inevitable product of unbelief. The problem with fascism and communism, however, is not that they are too critical of religion; the problem is that they are too much like religions. Such regimes are dogmatic to the core and generally give rise to personality cults that are indistinguishable from cults of religious hero worship.
> ("10 MYTHS – AND 10 TRUTHS – ABOUT ATHEISM"
> <www.edge.org/conversation/10-myths-mdash-and-10-truths-mdash-about-atheism> accessed January 5, 2020)

Another cogent rejoinder from Dawkins includes his observation, "What matters is not whether Hitler and Stalin were atheists, but whether atheism systematically influences people to do bad things. There is not the smallest evidence that it does" (*The God Delusion* 309).

In this book, I gathered examples of comedians and other humorists who occupy the center of my a Venn diagram (1.1) based upon the observation that some comedians seemed more interested in religious satire after the horrific events of September 11, 2001. Comedians such as Bill Maher, Ricky Gervais, and writer A. J. Jacobs explicitly used their platform as humorists to push back against religious extremists. Furthermore, this corresponds with a rise in secularism and atheism, a cultural Zeitgeist including but not limited to the umbrella term New Atheism. Some comedians such as Maher, Paul Provenza, Ian Harris, and Julia Sweeney are clearly activists in this movement, while others seem to champion rationalism, secularism, and science, even if they were not actively engaged in New Atheist-esque culture wars. Examples of pro-rationality comics include all of the ones already named as well as Jim Jefferies, Eddie Izzard, and Brian Malow, and many more. All of these artists intentionally and effectively create this increased public profile for rational thinking. If comedians are the new public intellectuals, then these comedians are on the vanguard of the struggle for voice, for recognition, and for the politics of reason.

Perhaps, these dates serve as bookends that help focus my investigation: between September 11, 2001, and June 4, 2016 (the date of the second Reason Rally), one can identify numerous examples of the zeitgeist I am excavating. Gary Wolf's 2006 essay coins the term, New Atheist, and between 2004 and 2007, the so-called four horsemen of the apocalypse (Dawkins, Hitchens, Harris, and Dennett) release their five key books. But also, important examples in comedy occur. Most notably, Maher's film *Religulous* is released in 2008, but other relevant examples include Lewis Black's 2002 *Comedy Central Presents* (as well as that entire season of *CCP*), the launching of Maher's

Conclusion 71

HBO show *Real Time*, and comedy specials by Izzard, Gervais, Minchin, and Maron.

One must remember that there are literally hundreds of comedy clubs across the United States, plus untold smaller venues, one-nighters, and open mics, the art of live stand-up happens in rooms large and small, in seemingly every city and certainly every state. Live comedy is the hidden portion of the iceberg contrasted with the higher profile media platforms top comedians utilize. From late-night comedy to panel shows, from comedy specials to podcasts, these various streaming, televisual, and audio media comprise the higher profile and more culturally available forms of stand-up comedy. Between the internet, streaming services, and podcasts, at this point, there are thousands of such variations. But outside the Stephen Colberts and Bill Mahers of the world, most live stand-up exists at levels below massive popular consumption. All of this is to sketch a picture that the majority of stand-up comedy is transient, invisible, and highly varied. One would never be able to document stand-up comedy in its fullest, twenty-first century expression. And no trend is omnipresent nor absolute.

This is not only a veritable ocean of artistic output, but, like all live performing arts, it is gone forever simultaneously with the moment of its occurrence. This means that one may never be able to narrowly calculate a quantity of religious satire, nonetheless one necessarily could find examples of stand-up comedians who function at the intersection of the Venn diagram which motivates this work. Three overlapping worlds: New Atheism, September 11, and contemporary religious satire. Some comedians do relatively modest examples of religious jokes, often akin to roasting cultural assumptions and practices. These types of jokes are gentler and less potentially offensive than the charged comedy of Maher, Gervais, and Black. To one degree or another, these comedians and others like them are actively pushing back against the hypocrisy and the danger of religious movements with society today. They are actively pro-science, pro-skepticism, pro-secularism, and actively anti-dogma, anti-hypocrisy, and anti-pseudoscience. (In reviewing the performers who seem to be participants in this zeitgeist I have identified, there is a feeling that seems to oscillate back and forth between prescriptive and descriptive forces. Am I describing how it has been done or recommending how to do it?)

Calls for mocking believers and any anti-rational elements in organized religion were clearly a feature of New Atheism. At the 2012 Reason Rally, Richard Dawkins used the Catholic ritual of the Eucharist as an example. He urged people to ask, "Do you really believe that when a priest blesses a wafer it turns into the body of Christ? Are you seriously telling me you believe that? Are you seriously saying that wine turns into blood?" Then, he went one step further, "Mock them! Ridicule them! In public!" Though aggressive-sounding, there is an underlying tenet – that religion should not be exempt from rational public discourse. Humorist Douglas Adams lamented that religion does not seem admitted to the sphere of public debate.

> Religion doesn't seem to work like that; it has certain ideas at the heart of it which we call sacred or holy or whatever. That's an idea we're so familiar with, whether we subscribe to it or not, that it's kind of odd to think what it actually means, because really what it means is "Here is an idea or a notion that you're not allowed to say anything bad about; you're just not. Why not? – because you're not!"
>
> ("Is there an artificial God?")

Ken Ham of the Tabernacle of Ignorance Creation Museum reacted to the 2016 Reason Rally by reportedly claiming that atheists are "putting their hands over eyes and ears and shouting 'I refuse to hear and see the truth'." No report yet on whether or not Ham is irony-impaired.

Stand-up comedians use their on-stage personas as a platform to provide insightful observations and to perform outraged reactions (a la Chili Challis's model of character-based premises and punch lines). In the case of religious satire, they collect observations about religious claims, dogma, and hypocrisy and through the craft of exaggeration lampoon bad ideas. This comic exaggeration exposes the fallacies or in some cases the outright dangers of some religious ideas or actors.

The more a religious leader demands their dogmatic notions be taken literally, the more they are exposed as "mechanical" in the Bergsonian sense. The literalness of the Creation Museum, of Evangelical prejudices, and even dangerous religious extremists and terrorists embody the Bergsonian aesthetic of the living being encrusted with the mechanical being one source of laughter. As P. Z. Myers put it, "religion is hilarious. It's a prime target for exposure of folly" (134–135). Hitchens also called it vain. In reference to those whose prayers and pleading to their all-maker seem ultimately self-aggrandizing, he wrote:

> Monotheists are supposed to pester their deity . . . lest he be deaf. How much vanity must there be concealed – not too effectively at that – in order to pretend that one is a personable object of a divine plan?
>
> (*God Is Not Great* 7)

As Bakhtin suggests, "However monologic the utterance may be . . . it cannot but be, in some measure, a response to what has already been said about the given subject . . . the utterance is filled with dialogic overtones" (in Morris, *The Bakhtin Reader* 86). Because of this, dogma can never be literally true. Rather, the meaning of biblical, Koranic, or other textual sources or utterances must be negotiated in real time and real spaces, between human interlocutors. This causes meaning to evolve in dialogic spaces. This can in some cases lead to solemn insights in theology or philosophy, or the modernization of some church's ideas – but this same situation leaves meaning open to hilarious interpretation based on word play, contrasting meanings, paradoxes.

In this sense, every religious utterance is like the duck-rabbit. One religious person may take a biblical passage and see a duck (aka what they consider "truth") while a comedian may see a very ridiculous joke-rabbit and point their comedic finger like a laser in an effort to get others to laugh at it. This is Maron's "lamb" in the creation museum, this is Black's description of 72 virgins, this is Jefferies "mysterious ways." Thus, authority may attempt monologic utterances, but meaning is ultimately dialogic.

As religious leaders attempt to portray biblical authority with dogmatic clarity, satirists exploit this inherent dissonance with anger, irony, and humor. It has been said that this type of humor is just preaching to the choir. That is surely not a fair critique. All public intellectuals have those who already follow and those who already dissent. But this does not stop anyone else from joining the debate. We cannot really know the effect of one speech, one idea, one good joke. On the other hand, the religious already preach to their choir, it works for them, why shouldn't the skeptic, the atheistic, and the satirist have the same right. There must be benefits, or churches wouldn't already do it.

Religious utterances are among the most monologic, making the whole genre prime for satire. And as Maron critiques the Museum on *This Has to Be Funny*, he also relishes the spirit behind the Museum, declaring with loving irony:

> But I left, not angry at them, not angry at the Museum, not angry at the people that were there. I was sort of elated, I felt sort of gloriously embarrassed for our country. But I felt deeply proud to be an American because I realized that what I was standing in the parking lot of could only happen in America. These are our fucking morons; and they've done a beautiful thing down there.

As Bill Maher put it:

> But there is a growing trend in this country that needs to be called out, and that is to label any evidence-based belief a religion. . . . Many conservatives now say that belief in man-made climate change is a religion. And Darwinism is a religion. And of course atheism, the total lack of a religion, is a somehow a religion too. According to the always reliable Encyclopedia Moronica. . . . You don't get to put your unreason on the same shelf with my Reason. Your stuff has to go over there, on the same shelf with Zeus, Thor, and the Kraken.

(*Real Time* February 3, 2012)

Additionally, it is clear that some of these comedians are intentionally responding to September 11. They intentionally champion critical thinking skills and science while beating back at the worst religious dogmas.

> God looked at them and said to himself, "They are so wicked, I will have to wipe them off the face of the Earth." Really? That's your only choice, is it? That's . . . You have to? Right . . . Straight to genocide. No one verbal and two written warnings? No? Just straight to the annihilation of the entire human race? Cause a fatty yellow-trousers picked someone's nose? That's your solution, is it? I mean, anger management. Chill the fuck out.
> (Ricky Gervais *Live 4: Science* (2010)

Of the comedians covered in this survey, it is well worth noting that there are perhaps two parallel categories. The first includes comedians who are consciously and actively participating in the New Atheism culture. This includes comics like Bill Maher, Ricky Gervais, Ian Harris, Paul Provenza, and Stephen Fry, and others. These comedians actively participated in projects and events with some of the leading thinkers of New Atheism.

Meanwhile, a second more stealthy and harder to categorize group of comedians also populates this study. This group includes artists who reacted to September 11 with an increasingly charged version of religious satire, even though they may not have had any connection to or interest in the Dawkins and Hitchens of the world. They were not consciously participating in the movement of New Atheism. And yet, they are undoubtedly participating in the post-September 11 zeitgeist of actively pushing back against religious extremism by an increasingly charged satire.

In terms of establishing this moment in culture, this mid-aughts rise in religious satire that seems to be a reaction to the religious extremism associated with the violence committed on September 11, the presence of both groups form an essential aspect of this analysis. Group one establishes a conscious connection; group two establishes the existence of the wider cultural moment. Furthermore, comedians in both groups engaged in satire that included all the rhetorical devices under review: Chapter 3's Doubting Thomas, Chapter 4's act outs designed to mock the incarnate, and Chapter 5's defense of science.

In Christopher Gilbert's "Of Satire and Gordian Knots," Gilbert wonders out loud if satire itself constitutes an attack on its audience. He characterizes the comedy of *The Onion*, Jon Stewart, and Stephen Colbert as damaging democracy and treating their audience as idiots. He characterizes Stewart as projecting "civic ignorance as a form of self-governance" and Colbert as portraying "affective attachment to sociopolitical realities . . . for the malcontents" (155). Rather than being corrective in sense of Fry, he brands them as postmodern in the damning sense and wonders out loud if they are but cynical "closed books." To him, they are self-congratulatory and preaching to an audience. He describes this situation as a "Postmodern conundrum" and a "Gordian knot" (128).

Of course, the Postmodern conundrum is that if texts are open to any even remotely variable interpretation, if Bakhtinian dialogue is always co-created, then Gilbert can be right in a rather meaningless way. He deconstructs these satirists in a similar manner as the comedians and comic writers described in this book are doing. Maron offers alternative readings of The Creation Museum, Gilbert offers alternative readings of contemporary satire. Perfectly valid, naturally so. Even so, the possibility that satirists promulgate ignorance is not core to the nuts and bolts work at hand. Provenza emphasized that most comedians do not define satire, they seek a joke that elicits laughter. As quoted above, Colbert said the same thing about the 2006 White House Correspondents' Dinner, making people laugh "matters to me" (27). Doubting Thomas's spread doubt, parody religions mock institutions, all while comedians pursue the ever-elusive laugh.

Select Bibliography

Baudrillard, Jean. *Simulacra and Simulation*. Trans. Sheila Faria Glaser. Ann Arbor: University of Michigan Press, 1994. Originally Published in French 1981.

Bergson, Henri. *Laughter: An Essay on the Meaning of the Comic*. Trans. Cloudesley Brereton and Fred Rothwwll. New York: Dover, 2005. Originally Published in French *Le Rire. Essai sur la signification du comique* in 1900.

"Bill Maher Performs 'Unbaptism' on Mitt Romney's Dead Father-in-Law." *The Hollywood Reporter*, February 3, 2012.

Caron, James E. "Satire Today: An Introduction to the Special Issue." *Studies in American Humor* 5 (1) 2019. 124–156.

Charlesworth, J. H. "Theodicy in Early Jewish Writings." *Theodicy in the World of the Bible*. Eds Antti Laato and Johannes C. de Moor. Leiden: Brill, 2003.

Chidestaer, David. *Authentic Fakes: Religion and American Popular Culture*. Berkeley: University of California Press, 2005.

Cowan, Douglas E. "'And Take Your Invisible Friend with You': Atheist Comedy and Religious Conversation (May Contain Offensive Language) [Special Issue: Religion and Humor]." *Bulletin for the Study of Religion* 42 (3) 2013. 32–36.

Dawkins, Richard. *The God Delusion*. Boston: Mariner Books, 2006.

Dennett, Daniel. *Breaking the Spell: Religion as a Natural Phenomenon*. New York: Penguin Books, 2006.

Dickinson, Tim. "Bill Maher on Palin, Pot, and Patriotism." *Rolling Stone*, Issue 1129, April 28, 2011: online. <www.rollingstone.com/politics/news/bill-maher-the-rolling-stone-interview-20110420>

Foucault, Michel. "Discourse and Truth: The Problematization of Parrhesia." (Six Lectures Given by Michel Foucault at Berkeley, October–November 1983, edited by Joseph Pearson). *Digital Archive: Foucault.info*, 1999: online. <https://foucault.info/parrhesia/about/> accessed December 27, 2019.

Frye, Northrop. *Anatomy of Criticism: Four Essays*. Princeton: Princeton University Press, 1957.

Garber, Megan. "How Comedians Became Public Intellectuals." *The Atlantic*, May 28, 2015: online. <www.theatlantic.com/entertainment/archive/2015/05/how-comedians-became-public-intellectuals/394277/>

Gilbert, Christopher. "Of Satire and Gordian Knots." *Studies in American Humor* 5 (1) 2019. 124–156.
Gournelos, Ted and Viveca Greene. *A Decade of Dark Humor: How Comedy, Irony, and Satire Shaped Post-9/11 America*. Jackson: University Press of Mississippi, 2011.
Harris, Sam. *Letter to a Christian Nation*. New York: Vintage Books, 2008.
Hitchens, Christopher. *God Is Not Great: How Religion Poisons Everything*. New York: Twelve Books, 2007.
Hitchens Christopher, Richard Dawkins, Sam Harris, and Daniel Dennett. *The Four Horsemen the Conversation That Sparked an Atheist Revolution*. New York: Random House, 2019.
Hofstadter, Richard. *Anti-Intellectualism in American Life*. New York: Alfred A. Knopf, 1963.
Holquist, Michael. *Dialogism: Bakhtin and His World*. London: Routledge, 1990.
Hutcheon, Linda. "The Politics of Postmodernism: Parody and History [Special issue: Modernity and Modernism, Postmodernity and Postmodernism]." *Cultural Critique* 5 (Winter) 1986–1987. 179–207.
Kirshenblatt-Gimblett, Barbara. *Destination Culture: Tourism, Museums, and Heritage*. Berkeley: University of California Press, 1998.
Kramer, Chris A. "Parrehisa, Humor, and Resistance." *The Israeli Journal of Humor Research* 2020. 22–46.
Lataster, Raphael. "A Superscientific Definition of 'Religion' and a Clarification of Richard Dawkins' New Atheism." *Literature & Aesthetics* 24 (2) 2014.
Lataster, Raphael. "The Argument from Evil, the Argument from Hiddenness, and Supernaturalistic Alternatives to Theism." *Religions* 13 (938) 2022: online. <https://doi.org/10.3390/rel13100938>.
Laycock, Joesph. "Laughing Matters: 'Parody Religions' and the Command to Compare [Special Issue: Religion and Humor]." *Bulletin for the Study of Religion* 42 (3) 2013. 19–26.
LeDrew, Stephen. *The Evolution of Atheism: The Politics of a Modern Movement*. Oxford: University of Oxford; Oxford University Press, 2016.
Maron, Marc and Brendan McDonald. *Waiting for the Punch*. New York: Flatiron Books, 2017.
Morris, Pam, ed. *The Bakhtin Reader: Selected Writings of Bakhtin, Medvedev, Voloshinov*. London: Arnold, 1994.
Most, Glenn W. *Doubting Thomas*. Cambridge: Harvard University Press, 2005.
Obeidallah, Dean. "Is It OK for Comedians to Joke About Religion?" *CNN*, January 10, 2015: online. <www.cnn.com/2015/01/09/opinions/obeidallah-comedians-religious-jokes/>.
Pojman, Louis P. *Philosophy of Religion: An Anthology*. Belmont: Wadsworth Publishing Company, 1987.
Raab, Scott. "Comedians as Prophets." *Esquire*, September 18, 2013: online. <www.esquire.com/entertainment/a24755/comedians-as-prophets-1013/>.
Samuelson, Heidi. "The Moment Where Your Laughter Becomes a Cackle: Pushing the Boundaries of Stand-Up Comedy." 2013 PCA/ACA Annual Conference.

Schechner, Richard. *Performance Theory*. New York: Routledge, 1988.
Shermer, Michael. *Why People Believe Weird Things*. New York: St. Martin's Griffin, 1997 (reprinted 2002).
Smith, Chris. *The Daily Show (the Book): An Oral History*. New York: Grand Central Publishing, 2016.
Spicer, Robert N. "Before and After *The Daily Show*: Freedom and Consequences in Political Satire." *The Daily Show and Rhetoric: Arguments, Issues, and Strategies*. Edited by Trischa Goodnow. Plymouth, UK: Lexington Books, 2011.
Volosinov, V. N. *Marxism and the Philosophy of Language*. Trans. Ladislav Matejka and I. R. Titunik. Cambridge: Harvard University Press, 1973.
Waisanen, Don, Hershey H. Friedman, and Linda Weiser Friedmann. *What's So Funny About Arguing with God? A Case for Playful Argumentation from Jewish Literature*. Dordrecht: Springer Science + Business Media, 2014: online. <https://link.springer.com/article/10.1007/s10503-014-9316-4>.
Webber, Julie. *The Cultural Set Up of Comedy: Affective Politics in the United States Post 9/11*. Chicago: Intellect, 2013.
Weisenburger, Steven. *Fables of Subversion: Satire and the American Novel*. Athens: University of Georgia Press, 1995.
Wild, David. "Checking in with Bill Maher (in 1999): After Monica, the 'Politically Incorrect' Host Gets to the Real Issues: Super-Model Slights, Howard Stern's Jealousy and the Importance of Jesse Ventura." *Rolling Stone*, April 13, 2011: online. <www.rollingstone.com/culture/news/checking-in-with-bill-maher-in-1999-20110413#ixzz48ve3deA4>.

Index

Adams, Douglas 72
Alm, Nico 46
Answers in Genesis 55, 56, 59
Aristocrats, The 14
Aristophanes 12, 13, 14, 45
Athens 1
Axis of Evil, The 11

Bakhtin, Mikhail 16, 17, 18, 20, 21, 46, 59, 62, 68, 72, 75
Barr, Rosanne 22
Baudrillard, Jean 34, 38, 58, 59
Benign Violation Theory 22
Bergson, Henri 20, 21, 57, 58, 61, 62, 72
Black, Lewis 1, 2, 9, 61, 67, 70, 71, 73
Borat 17

Caeser, Sid 61
Carlin, George 7, 20, 21, 33, 40
Caron, James 32
Carter, Judy 38
Center for Inquiry, The 66
Challis, Chili 57, 62, 72
Chapman, Graham 41
Charlesworth, J.H. 25
Charlie Hebdo 43
Chidester, David 5, 45
Church of the Flying Spaghetti Monster 44, 45, 46, 52
Cleese, John 40
Clouds, The 12
Colbert, Stephen 2, 13, 14, 23, 35, 48, 71, 74, 75
Colbert Report, The 13, 14, 48

Comedy Central Presents 1, 21, 29, 67, 70
Comical Heathen Podcast, The 11, 15, 17, 23, 65, 67
Cook, Dane 38
Cowan, Douglas E. 9
Creation Museum 9, 19, 20, 54, 55, 57, 58, 59, 61, 62, 72, 75
Crenshaw, James L. 29

Daily Show, The 2, 35
Danson, Ted 22
Darwin, Charles 23, 49, 50
Davies, Edward 47, 48
Dawkins, Richard 3, 4, 6, 15, 27, 46, 47, 57, 64, 65, 66, 68, 69, 70, 71, 74
"Dear God" 49, 50
Dennett, Dan 3, 4, 5, 70
DeRosa, Joe 43
dialogic 17, 18, 19, 20, 23, 25, 58, 59, 62, 72, 73
Dickinson, Tim 33
Dion, Dan 14
Dobbs, Lou 6
Doubting Thomas 8, 25, 29, 30, 31, 36, 37, 48, 74, 75
Dratch, Rachel 51
D'Souza Dinesh 69
duck-rabbit 34, 72
Dunham, Jeff 10

Earthquake 29
Ehrman, Bart 13, 25, 27
evolution 9, 20, 23, 45, 55, 60, 63, 64

Falwell, Jerry 1, 2
Foley, Dave 48
Foucault, Michel 32
Friday Night, Saturday Morning 40
Frye, Northrup 15, 21, 30, 31, 35, 58, 69
Fry, Stephen 4, 25, 74
Fudd, Elmer 8
Futurama 19

Gaffigan, Jim 21
Galifianakis, Zach 1
Garber, Megan 32, 35
Gervais, Ricky 5, 23, 24, 37, 38, 40, 65, 66, 70, 71, 74
Gilbert, Christopher 16, 74–75
Gilbert, Johanna 20
Goldberg, Whoopi 22
Greenberg, Jonathan 48
Green Room, The 14
Griffin, Kathy 22
Grossman, Cathy Lynn 66

Ham, Ken 54, 55, 56, 59–60
Harris, Ian 15, 16, 66, 70, 74
Harris, Sam 3, 4, 10, 25, 55, 64, 68, 70
Henderson, Bobby 45
Hicks, Bill 33, 61
Hitchens, Christopher 3, 5, 6, 9, 64, 68, 70, 72, 74
Holquist, Michael 17, 59
Holy Land Experience, The 33
Hooper, Simon 7, 23, 60
Humor Code, The 22
Humor Research Lab 22
Hutcheon, Linda 13, 44, 47

Ince, Robin 61, 63
Intelligent Design 9, 64
Islamophobia 10
Izzard, Eddie 5, 9, 25, 27, 28, 38, 39, 40, 42, 61, 64, 70

Jacobs, A. J. 70
Jaffe, Marc 14
Jefferies, Jim 5, 28, 29, 57, 64, 70, 73
Jonson, Ben 7

Kaplan, Gabe 61
Kattell, Steven 3
Kennedy, Dwayne 67
Kierkegaard, Soren 5
Kirshenblatt-Gimblett, Barbara 58
Knights, The 12
Kramer, Chris A. 32
Kreftling, Rebecca 21, 22
Kreps, Daniel 50, 51
Kuipers, Giselinde 2

Larson, Bob 48
Last Week Tonight 50
Lataster, Raphael 6, 26
Laycock, Joseph 46, 52
Leifer, Carol 21
Leno, Jay 2
Letterman, David 2
Lewis, Richard 61
Lichter, S. Robert 2
Life of Brian, The 8, 40, 41
Limbaugh, Rush 41, 43
Lord, Leighann 17, 65–66
Louis C.K. 41, 42, 43
Lysistrata 12, 45

Maher, Bill 3, 5, 8, 10, 21, 30, 31, 33, 34, 35, 36, 38, 39, 42, 44, 47, 48, 54, 59–60, 61, 66, 70, 71, 73, 74
Malow, Brian 65–66, 70
Maron, Marc 9, 15, 19, 28, 29, 42, 54, 56, 57, 58, 61, 62, 73, 75
Marx, Chico 17
Marx, Groucho 16
McGraw, Peter 15, 22, 23, 52
Measure for Measure 12
Minchin, Tim 5
Moliere 12, 13
monologic 17, 18, 19, 20, 23, 24, 25, 37, 46, 58, 59, 62, 72, 73
Monty Python 8, 40, 41, 42
Most, Glenn W. 30, 36, 60
Mother Teresa 26, 27
Muggeridge, Malcom 40, 41
Muslims Are Coming, The 11
Myers, P.Z. 27, 72

Nugent, Michael 47
Nye, Bill 66

Obeidallah, Dean 1, 42, 43
O'Brien, Conan 2
O'Donnell, Lawrence 48
Oliver, John 29, 44, 45, 50, 51, 52, 57, 60
Onion, The 2, 74
O'Reilly, Bill 13
Origin of Species 49
Oswalt, Patton 44, 52
Our Lady of Perpetual Exemption 44, 45, 50, 52, 57

palimpsest 19, 69
Palin, Michael 40
parrhesia 32
Penn and Teller 5, 66
Pojman, Louis P. 25, 27
Politically Incorrect 33
Provenza, Paul 5, 14, 20, 66, 70, 74, 75
Pryor, Richard 7, 33

Raab, Scott 30, 32, 35
Real Time with Bill Maher 3, 8, 23, 35, 47, 71, 73
Reason Rally (2012, 2016) 66, 70
Religulous 3, 9, 30, 31, 33, 35, 36, 44, 54, 59, 70

Safran, John 44, 45, 48, 49, 50
Schaeffer, Christopher 46, 68
Seinfeld 15, 38, 40
Seinfeld, Jerry 38, 68

Shakespeare, William 7, 12, 13, 14
Shermer, Michael 14, 64, 66, 69
Silverman, David 66
Silverman, Sarah 5, 22
Simpsons, The 16
Singer, Ryan 62
Spicer, Robert N. 35
Springsteen, Bruce 8
Stanhope 57
Stewart, Jon 2, 35, 74
surplus of vision 18, 19, 21
Sweeney, Julia 66, 70
Swift, Jonathon 45

Tartuffe 12
Tate, Geoff 62
theodicy 8, 9, 25, 26, 27, 28, 37
Tyson, Neil De Grasse 65, 66

Waisanen, Don 21
Warner, Joel 22
Weatherly, Michael 22
Webber, Julie 47, 48
Weisenburger, Steven 31
Williams, Robin 8, 38
Wolf, Gary 4, 68, 70

XTC 49, 50

Yaqhubi, Zohra D. 39
Yentl 48
Youngman, Henny 68
Young Turks, The 48

Zaltzman, Andy 29

For Product Safety Concerns and Information please contact our EU representative GPSR@taylorandfrancis.com
Taylor & Francis Verlag GmbH, Kaufingerstraße 24, 80331 München, Germany

www.ingramcontent.com/pod-product-compliance
Lightning Source LLC
Chambersburg PA
CBHW051800230426
43670CB00012B/2365